The Well of the Heads

And Other Tales of the Scottish Clans

by

Stuart McHardy

Birlinn

First published in 2005 by
Birlinn Limited
West Newington House
10 Newington Road
Edinburgh
EH9 1QS

www.birlinn.co.uk

ISBN 10: 1 84158 385 5
ISBN 13: 978 1 84158 385 3

British Library Cataloguing-in-Publication Data
A catalogue record for this book is available from the British Library

Typeset by Hewer Text UK Ltd, Edinburgh
Printed and bound by Creative Print and Design, Wales

To all those whose hearts are in the Highlands

Contents

Introduction

In the Highlands of Scotland till modern times there lived a warrior-society that in many ways resembled those that flourished all over Europe in the Iron Age over two thousand years ago. Focused on the central role of the warrior, the Scottish clan system, built round the ties of blood, continued to exist alongside the modern rapidly industrialising society of eighteenth-century Britain. The clans were united by claims of common descent from a distant ancestor and such ancestors could have been Picts, Scots or even Norsemen – the peoples who roamed first millennium Scotland. The warriors of the clan, fiercely loyal to each other and to the chief, the centre of all clan life, were known for their remarkable courage and endurance, selfless loyalty and highly developed military skills. Not for nothing were they considered the best fighting men in the world. These skills in time formed the backbone of the British armies that conquered the world – the Highland regiments.

The tales collected here illustrate the drama and dynamism of a society that lived close to nature, had little in the way of material wealth but was possessed of an intellectual treasure-house of story and song. That tradition gives us instances of outstanding bravery and cold-hearted deceit, loyalty to the death and the eeriness of the magic and the supernatural.

There are also a couple of stories of clan origin, 'A Grand Archer' being a direct echo of the ancient Norse myth of Orvandel, while the 'Son of the Carpenter' illustrates the roughness of humour that can exist in traditional material. The stories

1

were told round the peat fires of the Highland clans and in many Lowland areas, and served for both entertainment and moral education. Young men learned how to behave, and how not to behave, through such stories. These stories make no claim to being historically accurate. As an example of what can happen, the story of the Battle of Harlaw eventually gave rise to the ballad that claimed that 40,000 men came from the Western Isles, an impossibly large number. Many of these stories might similarly have exaggerated the numbers of warriors involved, but this does not matter. The telling of the stories was an integral part of both Gaelic-speaking and Scots-speaking societies and derived from much older traditions amongst both the Gaelic-speaking Scots and the Picts, who spoke a language akin to Old Welsh.

While historians obsess about the written word – though increasingly it is becoming obvious that much of Scotland's supposed early documentation has been 'adjusted' for propaganda purposes – the storytellers respected what we might call the psycho-sociological realities that underpin the stories. Stemming from ancient traditions that flourished for millennia without the written word, the stories here give us pictures of an ancient, essentially tribal society that lived in tandem with the emerging modern world.

Much of the material here, as befits a society in which every able man was a warrior, revolves around battle and raiding. Every man was a warrior, but warriors are not soldiers and the men of the clan had ties of blood to the men who led them. They were not linked to their leaders by feudalism but by kinship relationships that had survived intact for incredible lengths of time. Some of these stories concern women of the clans, and it is hardly surprising that they too became involved in battle. Women were always respected in Highland society, though as ever there were exceptions to the general behaviour. Just as there were always men whose self-interest led them to breaking the honour code, so there were men whose lust overpowered whatever sense of decency they might have had. There are tales here of revenge, the dish best served cold. There are also instances of blood-chilling cruelty as in 'The Smooring of the MacDonalds'. However, when we see the remarkable loyalty that could exist within clans, and the remarkable sense of honour and fairness shown in the story 'Real Highland Hospitality', it is difficult to credit the later government-driven propaganda depicting the Highlander as a thieving savage.

The figure of the Highland warrior, and particularly that of the clan chief, has been the subject of a great deal of Romantic wishful-thinking over the years. They lived in a society that was perhaps an anachronism even by the the eighteenth century, but for those born into it, this was all the world they knew. Hopefully these tales will entertain and help give a picture of what was the last Celtic-speaking warrior society in Europe. By understanding that society better we might yet develop a truer picture of the real history of Scotland.

Edinburgh, 2005   Stuart McHardy

Highland Honour

Real Highland Hospitality

Now for as long as people could remember the Highlanders had
loved to hunt. While in the olden times the favourite target would
have been the wild boar, a truly ferocious and fearless beast,
whose indomitable spirit saw it used as a warrior symbol in many
societies, by the Middle Ages it had been hunted to extinction.
The main target for hunters then became the red deer, beloved
of the kings of Scotland as well as the warriors of the Highland
clans. Even to this day, stalking for red deer plays a considerable
part in the economy of many Highland estates. Although they
enjoyed the hunt, it wasn't just for sport and it was long believed
in the Highlands that venison was good for you, especially if you
were ill or had been wounded. It also provided a considerable
part of most people's diet. The importance of deer in Highland
society can be seen in the stories of the great hero Finn Mac-
Coul, which formed a central part of Highland Gaelic lore. His
original name was Demne, which some think meant little deer;
his wife Sadv was turned into a deer by a malevolent Druid and
their son was called Oisin, or Ossian, which meant fawn.

From an early age Highland lads were instructed in hunting
the deer and many of them were addicted to the thrill of the
chase. One time a couple of Lamonts from Castle Toward in
Cowal were hunting in Forest of Etive. One of them was the son
of the chief of the Lamonts who had not long come to manhood.
They were heading towards Inverlochy when they met up with

the son of MacGregor of Glenstrae and a couple of his friends who were also out hunting. Neither group had had much luck so they decided to try their hand together. The day proved fruitless and that evening the five of them ended up at Kingshouse Inn in Glencoe. What happened next has never been satisfactorily explained, but somehow the two young men fell out. They exchanged words. One thing led to another, and finally young MacGregor lay dead on the floor from a blow by Lamont's dirk! At once Lamont took to his heels and ran off into the hills.

He travelled through the mountains in the hours of darkness, sure that MacGregor's companions would be hot on his heels and in the morning before dawn had streaked the sky he came down into Glen Strae, through which the river runs into the northern waters of Loch Awe. He had made remarkable time over rough ground in the dark and was close to exhaustion. Seeing a light shining from a nearby house he went to the door and knocked. When it was answered by a fine-looking, older man he asked for hospitality and protection.

'Aye, I will give you hospitality and you will be under my protection till tomorrow morning, come what may,' said the older man. So Lamont was taken into the house and given food. Soon the household was astir, and presently there was another knock at the door, which was again answered by the older man himself. There stood a group of MacGregors, faces drawn, come to tell their chieftain that his son had been killed by Lamont. For the young Cowal lad had come direct to the door of Glenstrae himself, the father of the man he had killed! Behind Glenstrae his wife and daughters heard the news and burst into lamentations. Their cries grew even louder when the men at the door said they had trailed Lamont to the chief's house. Glenstrae had given hospitality and protection to the killer of his own son.

'Let us have him,' cried one of the men at the door.

'No, he is my guest,' came the reply in a voice cracking with grief.

5

'But he has killed your son,' came another voice.

'Let no one hurt a hair on this lad's head,' the words came slowly, 'for MacGregor has given his word. He shall be safe while he remains under my roof. Now go.'

The house was filled with keening and crying and the womenfolk tried to persuade Glenstrae to hand over the young Lamont to his men. But he was adamant. The rules of Highland hospitality were one thing and the word of the MacGregor was another. No matter the horror and despair in is heart, he would not go back on his word. His son's body was brought back and a great funeral was held, and all the while Lamont was inside the chief's house. The clan seethed against the Cowal man, but there was nothing to be done, although many wished to do something. And so it was that one day soon after, just as the dawn broke, Glenstrae came out from his house fully armed, with Lamont at his side. Both men were prepared for a considerable journey, and under the watchful eyes of a couple of dozen armed MacGregors, their chief led the killer of his son away. They passed down through Glen Shira with never a word spoken between them. They reached Dundarave Point on Loch Fyne where MacGregor procured a boat for Lamont to row over to Cowal. As the young man got into the boat MacGregor spoke: 'I have fulfilled my vow. Once you are on the other side you are no longer under my protection and I can defend you no longer. You will have to take your own chances. Flee for thy life and may God forgive you for what you have done.'

And the old man turned away broken-hearted, to take the road home. Lamont rowed like a madman, and once on the other side he made as fast a pace as he could till he gained the security of his own lands round Castle Toward. Never again did he stray far from his own home, as he knew that the MacGregors roamed far and wide and that there was no chance they would forget him! As for Glenstrae, he lived on for many years, and into the time that the whole country seemed to have turned against the MacGregors, from the king down. He was driven from his ancestral home and his kin were scattered to the winds. So it happened that old MacGregor found himself in the wild country of Cowal, alone and friendless.

One day he arrived at the door of Castle Toward and asked to see Lamont, by now chief himself. When Lamont asked who was asking to see him he was told, 'One who knows the Law of Hospitality.'

Realising who his visitor must be he ran down to the gate of the castle and brought the white-haired old man in to his home. It was here that MacGregor of Glenstrae spent his last days, under the protection of one he himself had saved, and when he passed on he was buried in the kirkyard at Cowal, far, far away from the lands of his MacGregor forbears in Glenstrae.

The Silver Spoon

In Glen Nevis there is a knoll near the old fort of Dun Dige called Cnoc na mi Chomairle, 'the Hillock of Evil Counsel'. The name comes from an incident that took place in the distant past. The people in the immediate area, the MacSorlies, who later became part of Clan Cameron, were much like all the other people of the time and their men were often involved in following the ways of the School of the Moon, in that they would go out in the long moonlit September nights to lift the cattle of distant clans. This raiding was generally in the country far to the east over the mountains, and the people they raided were often members of the Clan Chattan. This was a confederation of various clans encompassing the Davidsons, the Farquharsons, the Mackintoshes, the MacPhersons, Shaws and others. Over the generations the MacSorlies and the Clan Chattan were often at odds and had come to see each other as traditional enemies. Now at the time we are looking at the chief of the MacSorlies decided that the situation was intolerable. Any time any of his men met with a member of Clan Chattan there was a fight and too many of his clansmen were being killed in what he thought of as essentially pointless battles. It was getting to the stage where it was impossible for any of the MacSorlies to go into Strathspey or further east without trouble.

He therefore resolved to invite a number of the leading men of Clan Chattan to come to Glen Nevis for a parley. He wished to come to a peaceful agreement with the Easterners. The day came, and the men of Clan Chattan, more than a dozen of them, comprising chieftains from a variety of different clans, came to Dun Dighe. They were given the very best of hospitality and all day long discussions went on. There were many old scores brought up and negotiations were at times very delicate, but the Clan Chattan men saw some sense in what MacSorlie was suggesting. Both sets of clansmen knew they would never be able to exclude the possibility of some of their number raiding the others' cattle but the endemic hostility between the two clans was clearly of no benefit to anyone.

At last, as the evening drew on, agreement was reached and hands were shaken all round. As the Clan Chattan men prepared to leave and cover a few miles before darkness, MacSorlie called on his piper to play them off with a tune. It is said that the tune he decided to play was a fateful one indeed. He played the traditional rallying tune of the Camerons, 'Sons of the Dogs come here and get Flesh'. This was immediately taken as an insult by the men of Clan Chattan, whose symbol of course was the cat.

Dismissing his piper with heavy words MacSorlie tried to placate the Clan Chattan men. 'You have my word,' he pleaded, 'no insult was meant to any of you at all. That piper is just a stupid and arrogant fool. We have done well here today by agreeing a peace. Please do not allow the actions of one stupid oaf to undo all that we have achieved here today.'

His words fell on deaf ears. Like Highland warriors throughout the centuries the Chattan men, feeling their honour had been insulted, would brook no apology. The sense of Highland honour was closely intertwined with each individual's sense of himself, and pride, once offended, precluded the possibility of apology. So, muttering words of vengeance about to come, the Clan Chattan men set off eastwards. Having invited them onto his lands and given them hospitality, they were under MacSorlie's protection by the code of the Highlands so he had little choice but to watch as his enraged guests headed off. The MacSorlies, though they greatly outnumbered the Clan Chattan deputation, could only stand by as the angry group headed off. They did not go far, and very soon afterwards they stopped on the knoll, watched by a group of MacSorlies from a distance.

The first to speak was Uilleam Farquharson from Deeside: 'Well, we have two choices,' he said. 'We can head back home and gather up more of the lads and come back and let these damned MacSorlies pay the price of insulting the men of Clan Chattan.'

'Aye,' Ewan MacPherson burst in, 'Let's get as many lads as we can and come back and wipe out these scum . . .'.

'Och, hold on now Ewan,' interjected Callum Shaw, a grey-haired warrior in his late forties and the oldest of the men present, 'I am thinking that Uilleam has something more to say. Isn't that right Uilleam?'

Farquharson smiled grimly, 'Aye. As I was about to say Ewan, we can go back for more of the lads or we can head back homewards for a bit and come back tonight. MacSorlie and his whelps will not be expecting that now, will they?'

There were muttered words of approval as the group on the knoll thought this over. It was only a matter of minutes before all had agreed and the party of warriors headed off towards the east, followed for a few miles by a larger group of MacSorlies. However, as night was falling, the MacSorlies, certain that the Clan Chattan men were well on their road home, turned back towards their own homes. They knew well that the Clan

Chattan men would seek vengeance for the insult but had been fooled into thinking that they had time to prepare for the eventual attack. They headed back to Dun Dighe and told MacSorlie that the enemy had left their lands.

However, it wasn't long before the warriors of the Cat were backtracking towards Dun Dighe. MacSorlie, accepting that they had headed back east, had posted no sentries, so under the cover of darkness and in complete silence the men of Clan Chattan fell on the clachan at Dun Dighe. Creeping silently into the houses they slit the throats of every man, woman and child they could find, including the chief and all his immediate family! But one of the chief's sons heard something and awoke to find himself surrounded by the Clan Chattan men, managing to raise a shout before he was struck down. The few of his relatives still living were alerted and took to the hills, while behind them the houses of the clachan burst into flames.

Amongst the MacSorlies who got away was young Iain, the chief's son, who was taken off by one of his father's oldest battle companions, Torquil Mor. Realising what had happened as he awoke in the night in the chief's house Torquil had grabbed the infant and a handful of heirlooms from the kitchen before escaping through a window. As he headed into the hills he turned to look back at the clachan at Dun Dighe. Each and every house, including the fine big hall where he had spent so many grand nights with his chief, were all ablaze. Still he had no time to mourn; he had to make sure the young chief was safe, so he headed up into the hills.

The Clan Chattan men headed home in the night, leaving the clachan at Dun Dighe ablaze with the bodies of several dozen MacSorlies lying dead in their own beds. There never were very many members of the wee clan and this sorely reduced their numbers. Only a week or so later the Easterners returned with a much larger force and hunted down as many of the MacSorlies as they could find. Many of them were forced to take to the hills to survive as the raiding party set about firing their houses and lifting all the cattle and other goods they could lay their hands on.

Now Torquil knew that his first duty was to keep the young lad alive. The youngster was not much more than eighteen months old at the time and the pair of them lived frugally in the hills for almost two years. Torquil, like most Highlanders, could live pretty well off the land when he had to, and he was careful not to let even the other MacSorlies in the area know that he had saved the chief's son. After a couple of years, having passed the winters with an old aunt who lived alone high in the hills above Glen Roy, he thought that the time was ripe to make his next move. As a result of living rough for all that time he was bit ragged-looking, and the lad himself was clad in little more than a scrap of plaid and animal skins. Thus the pair of them looked like beggars when they arrived at the door of Inverlair in Glen Spean. Here MacSorlie's sister, Beothag, lived with her husband's people the MacDonnels.

She had been devastated by the slaughter at Dun Dighe and had pleaded with her husband to revenge her on the men of Clan Chattan. This was not an action that he was prepared to take at the time, but ever since that fateful night relationships between the MacDonnells and the Clan Chattan had been growing steadily worse and she still had hopes that her people would be revenged. Because they had been such a small clan there were no other viable claimants to the chiefship and she had reluctantly accepted that the MacSorlies would simply be absorbed into the other clans in the area. As for Dun Dighe, the clachan there was left as it had been after the night-time raid on the MacSorlies.

So it was that one morning she came to her door to find a warrior with his plaid cowled over his head and with a wee lad at his heels.

'Good morning, lady, I was wondering if it might be possible for the lad and I to get something to eat,' the man asked.

She looked at the tattered pair before her and smiled sadly.

11

'Of course,' said she, 'there is plenty porridge here for you and
the wee lad; come on into the kitchen,' and led the pair into the
house. There she filled a big bowl of porridge from the pot on the
fire and put it down on the table where the man and the boy had
been shown to sit. She handed the bowl to the man and placed a
jug of milk on the table beside him. As he was still a toddler the
man clearly intended feeding the lad himself. She watched as he
reached inside his tattered plaid and pulled out a spoon which he
dipped in the porridge. It was a silver spoon. Puzzled a bit by
how this clearly poor man should have such a rare and valuable
item, she leaned over to look more closely. Just as the wee lad
took the first mouthful of the porridge she let out a gasp. She
knew that spoon. It had her grandfather's crest on it; it had been
in her family for generations and she herself had been fed with it
as a child. She drew back, her hand going to her throat, and let
out a cry. At once her husband and two other men ran into the
kitchen, all of them with their dirks drawn. At that the old warrior
seated at the table pulled the plaid from over his head, stood up
and bowed to Beothag.

'Oh my heavens, Torquil, is it you? And is this young Iain?'
her voice shook with a maelstrom of emotion. As Torquil
nodded the tears sprang from her eyes and she moved to pick
up the boy and clasp him to her breast.

MacDonell, looking on, knew what he had to do. He would
bring his brother-in-law's son up as his own. He would be
educated and trained as a chief and when the time came; well,
they would wait and see. As for Torquil, he would be well-
rewarded and given a place in his household for as long as he
lived.

So Iain was raised as if he had been one of MacDonnell's own
children. He was fostered out to a close relative of MacDonnell,
and at the age of seventeen he was told the full story of his birth
and early life. Soon after that he went with Beothag back to Glen

Nevis and with help of the MacDonnells the clachan of Dun Dighe was restored. The surviving MacSorlies, once they heard that the young chief had survived, flocked back to the area and once more they began to thrive. Over in the east the men of Clan Chattan heard that a son of the MacSorlie had reclaimed his father's heritage and knew that there would be a reckoning. But they knew also that he had been raised among the MacDonnells and they were reluctant to take them on. And after Dun Dighe was rebuilt, no MacSorlie would ever allow a cat inside it!

Origins

A Grand Archer

Now Malcolm Canmore was a great king, it is said. Not only did he rule wisely within the borders of Alba, he was known throughout Europe, maybe because his wife, the saintly Margaret, was herself of mixed English and Hungarian descent. Now kings have the habit of giving each other gifts as tokens of friendship, though sometimes it must be said such gifts were more in the way of distractions while devious plots were being laid; such is the nature of kings, such behaviour today being more the remit of politicians. However, one European king had given Malcolm a present of something that had never been seen or heard of in Scotland before. The story tells us it was a great beast which the local people considered to be akin to a frog or a toad, but from what we can tell it was probably a crocodile. Whatever the beast was it had a fearsome appetite and once the king had installed it on Eilean na Peiste – 'the isle of the beast' – in the River Don, he set about arranging for it to be fed. Such was its appetite that he placed a tax of one animal per croft per year on the countryside. Now this was a swingeing tax indeed, but for the widow MacLeod it spelt disaster. She had only the one cow, and the milk from it, combined with her careful husbandry of her garden, kept her alive. She had a son who helped her out, but he had a wife and a baby son of his own to feed and the widow was a fiercely independent woman. She was also possessed of a biting tongue.

One day, just after the announcement of the tax, her son came to visit. 'You claim to be of the blood of Torquil of the Eagles,' she spat at her son, reminding him of the eponymous founder of their clan, 'but there is no blood of the MacLeods in your veins, just water. You sit there by my fire while that Southron king takes the very food from my mouth. Call yourself a MacLeod warrior? Ochone, ochone what is to be become of me?'

MacLeod sat there silent under this tirade. Sure enough, he realised the situation. And his mother was right in what she was saying. What right had this Southron to come into their country and take the very food from the mouth of the poor? Nevertheless, he sat there saying nothing as his mother ranted and raged, till at last he went off into the night with her curses following him like a rabid dog. But he knew what he was about to do. Returning to his own house he quietly let himself in, listening to make sure his wife and child were sleeping. He then went to the place in the eaves where he kept his bow and quiverful of arrows. Like all men of his time he was a fully trained warrior, but he was known to be far and away the best archer for miles around. Stories were told that he could hit the eye of a fly at forty paces and bring down a twelve-point stag from half a mile away with his bow. He knew these stories to be a bit more than the truth, but he was sure of his skills, and steadfast in his intentions. Carefully unstringing the bow he wrapped the bowstring in greased cloth before putting it inside a well-greased leather pouch, which he slipped next to his skin inside his shirt. Then he headed off into the night, closing the door softly behind him.

He slipped through the night, down to the banks of the river opposite Eilean na Peiste and lowered himself into the freezing cold waters with as little noise as possible. With his quiver over his back and his bow in his teeth he swam swiftly out to the island. Once there he heaved himself ashore, and quickly pulling out the pouch with the still-dry bow-string in it he restrung his bow. He took two arrows from his quiver, notching one to the bowstring and gripping the other between his teeth. Then he began to move stealthily along the island which was no more than 50 yards long and about 20 to 30 yards wide. He smelt the animal before he saw it. Then he heard it move, and dropping to one knee in the faint moonlight he saw a great gleaming pair of eyes looking straight at him through the underbrush. Quick as a flash he sighted, drew and fired. His arrow flew straight into the left eye and a great roar erupted as the beast lurched back and fell over on its side. He had got it with his first shot. However, the noise had awakened the king's men who were guarding the beast on the banks of the river, and suddenly both banks were lined with armed men holding torches aloft. Boats were launched east and west of the island and MacLeod realised that escape was impossible. Still, he had done what he intended, and his mother would have food for the winter. As to what would now happen to his wife and child he dared not think.

MacLeod was taken prisoner and held in the dungeon of a nearby castle, till just a few days later, when the king had arranged to hold a justice moot on the nearby Gallows Hill. When MacLeod was brought before him the king was in no mood for mercy.

'You insolent pup. That creature was a royal gift from a great king from many hundreds of miles away over the sea and you thought you could just kill it as if it were one of your Highland wolves. Well you can think of how clever that was as you hang. String him up,' he said, snapping his fingers at a nearby officer of his guard.

'Ah, sire, can I have a word?' a voice came from his left side. It was Alan Durward, a close and trusted friend.

'What is it?' asked the king, holding his hand up as the officer stepped forward to take MacLeod off to the great gallows set up just a few paces away.

'Well, you see this MacLeod is just the best archer we have in the district and we have been relying on him for training up the young lads. And you know you were saying yourself just recently that we have need of more archers, sire,' said Durward gently. The king sat still, looking at MacLeod, his hands tied behind his back and held firmly by two of the guard. The young man looked straight back at him, head held high. Just then there was a commotion in the crowd nearby and a young woman clutching an infant to her breast burst from the assembled people. She ran forward and threw herself at the king's feet.

'Oh sire, please spare him. He is all I and my son and his poor old mother have in all the world; he is a dear, dear man, please sire . . .', and she burst into tears as her husband looked grimly on.

The king sat still for another minute, and then he spoke. 'Here is my judgement. You, MacLeod, are an archer of some repute it seems. So guards, take his wife and child over to the other side of the river and place a peat on her head. If you can shoot the peat off her head without harming either of them MacLeod, your life shall be spared,' and the king smiled, a wee grim smile. The watching crowd sucked in their breath. The river here was only 20 or 30 yards wide, but from here on the hillside the shot was more than 100 yards.

So the young woman and her child were taken across the river in a boat and a peat was placed on her head. She gathered all her strength and stood as straight and still as she could. Then MacLeod's bow and quiver were brought and at a nod from the king his bonds were cut. He reached out for his bow and flexed it a couple of times. The he reached to the quiver and took an arrow which he placed between his teeth before taking another arrow and notching it to the bowstring. The entire crowd fell silent.

MacLeod raised his bow, and just as he sighted the tiny peat on his wife's head, his hands began to shake. There was a great sigh from the crowd as he lowered the bow. The king smiled. Again MacLeod lifted the bow, but yet again his hand shook.

Again there was a great sigh from the crowd and the king's smile broadened. So this great archer was not up to the challenge. Well, he thought, he will just have to hang. He was just about to raise his hand and give the order when MacLeod whipped up the bow, sighted and fired more quickly than seemed possible. The arrow flew across the river and cleanly took the peat off his wife's head. The entire crowd erupted into cheering, and relieved of the bow and arrow MacLeod was brought to face the king.

'Well MacLeod, you have shown your skill with the bow right enough, and as I have said, you shall be spared. But tell me, what was the second arrow for?' he asked quizzically. The young man answered loud and clear, 'That sire, was for you if I missed or harmed my wife or son.' and there was great indrawing of breath from all the lords and soldiers around the king. How dare any man speak to the king like that! 'Well,' said the king, 'I can see you are a brave and honest man, and I daresay you might have managed to kill me despite the presence of my guard. I have need of men like you. Will you become one of my guard and swear to protect and serve me?'

MacLeod looked long and hard at the king. There was absolute silence as they all waited to hear what he would say.

'I am afraid I must refuse the honour, your majesty. After what you put me and my family through today I could not swear to be as loyal as you would require,' and as he said this, for the first time he bowed his head to the king. All around were stunned. The man had been given his life and now he was throwing the honour of being one of the king's guard right back in the king's face. Surely he must hang now!

Suddenly the king laughed. 'I see they breed their men tough up here right enough. You are as hardy a man as I have met in my life. You can go free, but from now on by order of the king you shall be called Hardy.' And from that day on it was as the king said, and in time the sons of the man born MacLeod became known as MacHardies.

Son of the Carpenter

In the Middle Ages much of the country of Scotland was still occupied by people living in clans whose way of life had in many ways remained unchanged for millennia. Like their far-distant ancestors they lived in closely knit family groups, herding the hardy black cattle of the Highlands and growing a limited range of foodstuffs. They were essentially self-sufficient, but through trade could acquire high-quality armaments and a limited range of luxuries from other parts of Britain and mainland Europe. By this period the clans were individually known by the name of some notable ancestor. Some of these names, like my own [McHardy], are said to have come about by bravery bordering on stupidity, and others, like Forbes, as a result of heroic battles against human or animal adversaries. There are other stories however, which tell of ancestors not just being brave but pretty smart with it.

One such tale concerns the MacIntyres, a clan who for many generations provided the hereditary pipers to the MacDonalds of Clanranald and the Menzies clans. They also seem to have had some sort of relationship with the MacDonalds' hereditary enemies, the Campbells. Strangely enough they had the right to the Clan Donald badge, the heath plant, and the clan Campbell war-cry *Cruachan!* Traditionally they occupied the lands around Glen Noe and Loch Etive, and like many of the western clans they were originally of Norse or mixed Norse–Gael ancestry. As it is, the difference between the Norse and the Gael would appear to have been more of language and culture than any variation in ethnicity. The name itself means 'the son of the Carpenter' and there are different versions of who this carpenter was. Some say he was a nephew of Somerled, the first Lord of the Isles, who saved his uncle's ship from sinking while others tell a different story.

That story is that the first of the MacIntyres was a MacDonald, either from Skye or the nearby mainland. Like all of the men of his clan he was as accustomed to travelling on water as on land, and he spent much of his life in his small boat off the coast. Somehow he broke the laws of his kin in a serious fashion, and in fact so bad was his misdeed that he was towed a long way out to sea in an old leaky boat and cast adrift. Before his companions left him they removed the bung from the hole in the bottom of the boat. Thus it would be only a matter of time before the boat would fill with water and he would be alone. His companions raised the sail in their own boat, and tacking into the onshore wind they were soon were a good way off. As soon as they had gone off a bit, he struck his left thumb in the bung hole.

From where he was the coast was below the horizon and so he would most probably drown long before he could swim ashore. Certainly his situation appeared hopeless, but as he bailed out some of the water with his right hand he thought, 'Where there's life there's hope.'

Having got rid of some of the water in the boat it became clear to him that his situation wasn't getting any worse, though he was aware, as all the people of the west coast were, that the weather could change very quickly. If a squall came up he would be finished but he refused to despair. Luckily the sea remained calm and the wind stayed relatively light from the shore. It might have been light but it was still slowly taking him ever farther from the shore and safety. He kept scanning the horizon every few minutes, and after a couple of hours he saw a sail further out to sea that seemed to be heading towards the shore. He had to attract the attention of the occupants, but he was crouched down in the bottom of the boat, held there by his thumb. If he removed it and they didn't see him, he was finished. But if he didn't succeed in alerting them he would be no better off. Something had to be done. Luckily he had managed to retain his *sgian dubh* when he had been manhandled onto the boat. With no hesitation he took the knife in his right hand and slashed right through the base of his left thumb. Stopping only to rip a piece off his plaid to staunch the bleeding, he then whipped off his plaid and whirled it round and round while shouting at the top of his voice. It wasn't long before he was spotted from the other boat.

The crew of the other boat, a considerably larger vessel, changed course and came to rescue him. They were men of another clan and when they saw just how had managed to bung the boat's hole they said that it was as fine a piece of carpentry work as they had ever seen. They then took him to their own lands further up the coast where they did what they could to treat his wound. Once the word went round the community of what he had done he was known to one and all as *an T-saoir*, the Carpenter, and so his descendants became the MacIntyres . . .

Native Intelligence

⟫◆⟪

The Sweetest Bite

Sir Ewen Cameron of Lochiel was the chief of Clan Cameron in the middle of the seventeenth century. From the age of twelve, he was brought up in the household of Campbell of Argyll who was a relation of his mother. Now Argyll was a leading Covenanter but Ewen always leaned towards being a Royalist, a sentiment that was greatly strengthened in 1645 when he watched the execution of the Royalist prisoners, captured at the Battle of Philiphaugh in Newark Castle, Selkirk. If Argyll thought this would bring young Lochiel into the Covenanting fold he was much mistaken. In fact Ewen had secretly met with a group of these, mainly Irish Catholic prisoners, and their courage in the face of their imminent execution made a lasting impression on him. So by the time he returned to lead his clan after the death of his grandfather Allan, he was firmly in the Royalist camp. Now although Argyll had had plans to have him educated at Oxford, Ewen had shown from an early age that he was a true Highland warrior and was what in modern terms would be called 'a man of action'. He was never loath to lead his clan in disputes with other Highland chiefs, and in the period between 1652 and 1669 he showed himself to be a master of Highland tactics in his battles with the Covenanters. The nature of such campaigning was essentially guerrilla warfare, a type of fighting that clan warriors were particularly suited to. In fact it might be fair to say that for many of the Highlanders there was

22

little difference between going to war and their traditional habit of cattle-raiding on other clans!

Now in 1654 Scotland was effectively under a military occupation by Cromwell's Protestant government in England, with General Monk in charge of the army. It had been decided to build a series of forts to try to control the Highland clans, many of whom were either Episcopalians or Catholics and supported the Stewarts' claim to the thrones of England and Scotland. One of these was at Inverlochy, in the shadow of Ben Nevis and Ewen kept a close eye on the construction. Such were the numbers of English troops sent to construct the fort that Ewen decided a full-scale assault on it was unlikely to succeed. However he kept a watching brief on the work, living in the nearby hills with a group of about thirty of his most trusted clansmen. One day a large working party came out in two ships up Loch Eil to get timber from the woods at Achdalie on the north side of the loch. Now the English troops numbered about 140, and they were armed with muskets. Ewen decided that with their broadswords, dirks, targes, bows and arrows as well as a fair number of muskets, the greatly outnumbered Camerons could gainfully attack this much larger force, as long as they had the advantage of surprise. Some of his clansmen were horrified at the suggestion. No Highland warrior would ever admit to fear, but the thought of attacking a force almost five times as large as their own struck them as utter madness. Ewen, however, was not to be dissuaded and such was the loyalty of the Camerons to their dashing young chief that the entire group accepted that they would just have to go along with him, even if he was mad! The government troops were strung out through the wood at Achdalie when with no warning they were attacked by the Camerons.

Now these government troops were trained soldiers and obeyed orders well. However, this proved to be their undoing, for, as the Camerons charged through the woods the order was barked out to fire. At once the troops raised their muskets and let loose a volley. Before they could reload the Camerons, taking advantage of the terrain in time-honoured fashion by charging downhill, were amongst them swinging with their swords and stabbing with their dirks. The English soldiers had bayonets on their muskets but these clumsy weapons were no match for the skill of the Highlanders with sword, dirk and targe. Although greatly outnumbered the Camerons cut down so many of the soldiers so quickly that the rest of them fled back towards Inverlochy.

At this point Ewen became separated from the main body of his clansmen and found himself up against an English officer who was determined not to run. He was a man of considerable courage himself and was intent on making this Highlander pay for the day's events with his life. Ewen was fit and strong, but his opponent was considerably bigger and stronger and no mean swordsman. Ewen's nimbleness, however, seemed to give him an advantage, and after a vicious bout of thrust, counter-thrust and parry he managed to deprive the officer of his sword. In an instant the Englishman threw himself at his opponent, catching Ewen off-guard and tumbling him to the ground. Holding tightly to each other they rolled down the slope, crashing through underbrush, bouncing off boulders and ending up in the bed of a stream which, given the conditions, was thankfully dry. Neither had any real strength left, but the advantage was with the Englishman as he was on top of his smaller and lighter opponent. Wrenching his right hand free from the Highlander's grasp the officer drew a dagger from a sheath in his belt and drew back to stab Locheil through the heart. Ewen grabbed at him, taking the Englishman's right hand with his own left, and as they struggled he gripped the collar of his enemy's coat with his left hand. Using the last of his strength he yanked his opponent down, and as the Englishman's throat came near he sank his teeth in it. Biting with all his force he ripped the throat from his enemy as he pulled himself back! As the dying Englishman fell back Ewen pushed

24

him off and spat out the flesh as the officer's lifeblood pumped out in a gory stream. He said later, 'Well, it was the sweetest bite I ever took in all my life, for without it I would have had no life at all!'

Getting to his feet he ran back to where his clansmen had chased the remnants of the troops back to where they had drawn up their boats on the shore of Loch Eil. There were still about thirty-five of the government soldiers still standing and as Ewen came close he shouted to his men to give them quarter. He thought that enough blood had been spilt.

Just as the Camerons fell back at this order one of the soldiers attempted to shoot Ewen, who saw what was happening and threw himself forward into the water as the shot whistled over his head. This incensed the remaining Camerons who once more fell on the Cromwellian troops and soon none were left. None that is except an officer who had managed to get out to one of the boats, and, resting a musket on the gunwale of the boat, aimed at Ewen and fired.

As the shot flew towards the Cameron chief, his foster-brother, a MacMartin of Letterfinlay, saw what was happening and threw himself in the way of the bullet. He was killed instantly and Ewen in a fit of blind rage forced his way through the water and killed the officer in the boat. Then he sadly took his foster-brother over his shoulder and carried the body all the way to his own family burial ground. It might have been 'the sweetest bite', and the Camerons lost only a handful of men for a notable victory, but it had come at the cost of foster-brother's life. It had long been noted that the bonds between foster-brothers were often even closer than those between brothers, and Ewen was heartbroken at his loss. But time is a great healer, and though he never forgot his foster-brother or his great sacrifice, the searing anguish of the loss did dull with time.

Many years later, when peace had been restored to the country, Lochiel was on a visit to London when he went into a barber's shop for a shave. After lathering his chin and just before he started to shave him the barber said to Locheil, 'You are from the north, aren't you sir?'

'That I am,' replied Locheil, 'Why, do you have relations up in Scotland?' 'Oh, no no sir,' the barber went on, 'it's just that there are some dreadful savages amongst them. I doubt a gentleman like yourself would believe it, but one of those barbarians ripped my father's throat out with his teeth. I tell you sir I only wish I had that scoundrel's throat as near as I have yours now. Damned savages.'

Tradition tells us that after this, Locheil never crossed the door of a barber's shop again!

Using the Head

Now Highland pride was a fierce and often deadly thing. In a society where every able-bodied man was a warrior and every man felt driven by his own sense of honour, most were very sensitive to what they might consider an insult. This could be a simple matter between two Highlanders fighting to the death over some perception of an unkind word, but sometimes the reaction to perceived insult could be something a bit more serious. In 1429, after a long struggle, James I had eventually managed to get the better of Alexander, Lord of the Isles, and had made the latter submit to him in public at Holyrood. Now the MacDonald Lords of the Isles were only nominally Scots, in that their loyalty, like most of the clans, was to their own kin and not the king sitting far off in Edinburgh. They claimed their descent from Somerled MacGillivray, a twelfth-century warrior of mixed Norse–Gael descent. The independence of all the clans was legendary and it is little wonder that the Highlands were not fully brought under the rule of government law until the mid-eighteenth century. Not that the Highlanders saw it like that; they had their own way of doing things, their own laws and customs, and they resented the imposition of what they saw as foreign ways by successive kings.

Now Alexander had been forced to submit because the king had managed to turn his allies in the Clan Chattan and Clan Cameron against him. Most of the clans were prone to considering what was best for their own people and the idea of a sense of loyalty to other clans beyond what was convenient was not one they would readily have understood. Today we tend to think of them as being united by their shared language, customs and history, but each kin-group's loyalty was to its own people first and foremost. So they could ally with the king or against him, depending on what the advantage for their own people appeared to be. This is the reason why so many Lowland commentators down the centuries have tried to portray the Highlanders as devious and dishonest: they simply marched to a different tune.

When Alexander submitted to the king many of the MacDonalds were angry and upset. And none more so than Alexander's cousin, Donald Balloch. He determined that this insult to his people could not go unavenged and gathered together a large force of men in the Hebrides. His intention was to conduct a widespread raid against the mainland, and as usual with the inter-tribal conflicts of Highland society, most of those supporting him were intending to come back with more than they left with! They landed in Lochaber in 1431 only to find a superior force awaiting them at Inverlochy under the joint command of the Earls of Mar and Caithness, who had advance word of their arrival. However, the MacDonalds were absolutely set on battle to avenge the insult they felt they had received, and they fell on the men of Caithness and Mar in a fury.

The battle was short and sharp and the MacDonalds were triumphant, Allan Stewart, the Earl of Caithness himself dying on the battlefield. Such was the rout of the troops loyal to the king that the Earl of Mar only got home after many weeks of being hunted as a fugitive throughout much of the Highlands.

Donald and his men now seized the opportunity of the enemy being in disarray and 'cleansed' the lands of the Clan Chattan and the Camerons in Lochaber, lifting as much livestock and moveable goods as they could manage. Realising however, that this precipitate action would force the king to come after him with an even larger force, Donald decided that for once discretion might be the better part of valour and sailed off to Ireland. Just as he had expected, King James raised a large army and headed for the Western Highlands, determined to subdue the MacDonalds for once and for all. Reports of the time say he came upon Lochaber like a roaring lion but all he found were chiefs who were as peacable as lambs. MacColl, MacNeill and MacAlister among others, readily came forward to submit to the king, all claiming *they* had had little or nothing to do with Donald Balloch's great raid. Not for the last time, the cry went up in Scotland 'it wisnae me!'. James, well aware that he was being lied to, but unable to find out where Donald Balloch was, found himself in a bit of a fix.

Here were all these Highland chiefs professing loyalty to him while the chief perpetrator of what he considered treason and rebellion had clearly fled the country. So he was in a quandary. He was not keen to stay in Lochaber any longer than necessary, but was unwilling to return without some resolution of the situation. Then one day while he was still there a birlinn was sighted off the coast sailing towards the area where the king was encamped. It came close to the land and a man stepped ashore carrying a bundle wrapped in a plaid. As he walked up the beach he unwrapped his bundle. It was the head of a mature bearded man, and at the sight of it, all the MacDonalds there began to weep and wail. Some of the fierce warriors fell to their knees and hammered the ground with their fists; others shouted at the sky with tears falling from their cheeks. 'Whose head is that?' demanded the king of one of the local chieftains. 'It is himself, Your Majesty, Donald Balloch,' the man replied.

James was delighted. This was just the resolution to the situation he had wanted. No more would he have to hunt for this wild man of the isles; now he could leave this wild and crude place and return to Holyrood and a decent lifestyle. Waiting only to hear the story that Donald Balloch had been killed in a duel with a distant cousin in Ireland the king gathered up his troops and returned south-eastwards to Edinburgh. In time Alexander was released from his imprisonment and restored to his position as Lord of the Isles. As for Donald, he had had to kill six different Campbells before he had one with exactly the right colour of hair and beard, and in later years he came back to become a thorn in the side of James's son and successor, James II.

The Tables Turned

The Comyns and the Mackintoshes were at feud throughout much of the fifteenth century. The chief of the Comyns at one point was appointed Keeper of Inverness Castle by the king, James I. Being the king's representative in the capital of the Highlands was a position of some power and he took full advantage of his position to have a bunch of Mackintoshes hung at Cnoc na Gillean, the Hillock of the Lads, near Nairn on the Moray coast. This of course drove the Mackintoshes into a fury and clearly vengeance was called for. A group of them under the leadership of their chief Malcolm, attacked Nairn Castle one evening while the Comyns there were eating, and with the advantage of surprise, slaughtered a considerable number of them.

This in turn incensed the Comyns and soon a force of 1,500 men had been gathered together to attack Malcolm's castle at Moy about ten miles south-east of Inverness. When Malcolm heard that such a force of Comyns was on their way he was in a bit of a quandary. He had only about 400 men to call on and realised that a pitched battle against such overwhelming numbers would be futile. To buy time he decided to take as many of his people as he could to the island in Loch Moy. The island had a small fortress, and although it would be crowded with the people from the immediate area, he reckoned that he could sit out the incursion by the Comyns there. So while some of the Mackintoshes went up into the hills to hide, Malcolm, his family and a large group of the people living round the castle rowed out to the island, making sure that there were no boats left anywhere around the shore of Loch Moy.

Coming over the Moor of Cawdor, the Comyns soon realised that the area was deserted, and when at last they reached Moy Castle it too showed no signs of life. It wasn't long before they noticed that there was a considerable number of people on the islet in the loch. Realising that there were no boats to mount a viable attack and that bringing any from elsewhere would be a complicated business with no guarantee of success – they would be picked off before they landed if they went out in small numbers – they discussed the matter and decided the best bet would be to starve the Mackintoshes out. This might take a bit of time, so one bright spark amongst them came up with the idea of raising the water-level of the loch and thus forcing the Mackintoshes off their island retreat.

'A grand idea that,' cried the chief of the Comyns, 'let's get to it lads.' So they started to build a dam across the spot where the Loch empties into the Funlack Burn. With the numbers they had it didn't take long, with some men felling trees, others cutting turf and a third group actually assembling the structure of the dam itself. To shorten the time needed some of the Comyns didn't even bother felling trees; they simply tore the roofs off some of the local *tigh dubh*, or dark houses of the Mackintoshes, and used their ran-trees or main rafters to hep construct the dam. Soon the waters of the Loch began to rise and the islet, only a couple of feet above the water line, was soon in danger of being flooded.

The immediate problem for Malcolm and his people was how to prevent their supplies of food and firewood from being soaked! Clearly something would have to be done or they would be forced to go ashore where the vengeful Comyns would be only too glad to welcome them. However, desperate times lead to desperate measures, and so it proved. As night fell Malcolm gathered together the most experienced of his clansmen, and by the light of a fire they discussed what options were open to them. There is an old saying that cometh the hour cometh the man, and sure enough that is just what happened.

One of the older warriors, Euan Mor had an idea:

'What if I take one of the wee boats and row down to the foot of the loch and take down the middle part of their dam?' he suggested, 'that way the waters of the loch will fall and we'll be safe, for a while anyway. There seems to be a lot of these damned Comyns around the dam and maybe the waters will rid us of some of them as well.'

'Do you think you can do it without being seen?' asked Malcolm.

'And can you be sure you can do it at all?' asked an old grizzled veteran of many skirmishes with the Comyns, 'they will likely have lookouts.'

'Aye, it's fell dangerous,' put in another, 'once you have started to destroy the dam they will likely hear you.'

'I have another idea there though,' declared another older man. 'What if you go and bore holes in the wood and plug them. You could attach the plugs to ropes and pull them out all together.'

'That might just work,' nodded Malcolm. 'Let's give it a go.'

So with as much rope and wood for plugs as he could carry, and with muffled oars, Euan Mor set off down the loch under the cover of darkness. All through the hours of the night he worked. Slowly but steadily he made holes through the structure where he could, inserted plugs and attached ropes to them.

It was hard work, all the more difficult as the only light came from the stars. Still he was happy there was no moon – he would have been spotted easily then. All the time he was keeping an ear, and an eye, open for any Comyn sentries. On two different occasions he had to stop work and hang in the water from the dam as he heard sentries walking by the dam. Luckily they were more concerned with keeping an eye on the island rather than the dam.

At last, not long before dawn, the holes had been drilled, the plugs inserted and Euan rowed back in his boat towards the island. Then taking a swig of whisky from a flagon he had with him, he started to pull on the various ropes dangling from the stern of his wee boat. One after another the plugs came free. The waters started to move, and as he was pulling the last of the plugs he felt the rush of the water pull his boat towards the dam. As the dam burst the waters surged and poor Euan was pulled down into the swirling debris as his boat overturned, and he was drowned in the swirling waters. He was not alone. Just below the dam, by the banks of the burn, a considerable number of the Comyns had made their camp. They were still sleeping, wrapped in their plaids when the waters burst on them, and before they knew what was happening they were inundated. Many of them were drowned as the waters surged and tumbled down the line of the Funlack Burn.

There was absolute uproar, with men screaming and others shouting, trying to help their comrades caught up in the flood. Such was the racket that most of the Comyns stationed around Loch Moy came running to the mouth of the Funlack Burn, there to see a scene of devastation. Malcolm and his men were keeping a lookout, and as soon as they saw a chance a bunch of them leapt into their boats and headed for the shore. There, after pulling their boats up from the shoreline to the underbrush, some of them waited in the woods while others ran to nearby locations where they knew other members of the clan were hiding out, awaiting developments. Once matters had been arranged to his satisfaction Malcolm signalled to a waiting clansman on the island and soon afterwards two more boats put out from the island and headed to where the earlier group had landed.

These boats were spotted by the Comyns at the Funlack Burn and a large party of them pursued the newly landed Mackintoshes. The Mackintoshes ran through the woods by the shore and up over the shoulder of a hill. The Comyns, furious at how their trick had been turned against them, were set on killing as many of their enemies as they could. So they ran up and over the shoulder of the hill, only to find a much larger group of Mackintoshes awaiting them. There on the hill above Loch Moy a vicious battle took place, with no quarter asked for or given, and it was a much depleted and sorry crowd of the Comyn clan who returned to their own lands the following day. The weight of numbers had been of no advantage, given the courage and commitment of Euan Mor Mackintosh and the fighting skills of his kin.

Donald Og

In the long dark nights of the Scottish winter the people of the clans liked nothing better than to sit by their peat fires and tell traditional tales. Some of these were of legendary figures from the past like Finn MacCoul; others were about the fairies and the supernatural, but one topic was always very popular. This was the story of the clan's finest fighting men. Each clan had its own favourite and some of these tales seem to have come from a period earlier than that in which they are set. The hero of one such tale was Donald Og Farquharson. A renowned swordsman, Donald Og was born on Deeside around 1630. Now by this time the chiefs and chieftains of the various clans were beginning to adapt to modern ways and some of them had become quite wealthy. In previous centuries wealth would have been calculated by the number of cattle and prestige by the number of fighting men in any clan, but now things were changing. With the Union of the Crowns of Scotland and England in 1603 the sons of chiefs and chieftains who in earlier times would have travelled extensively on the Continent, now began to go to London.

One time Donald Og went to that great city with a group of companions who included the current Lord Ogilvie and the Lairds of Pitfoddels and Drum. While these were powerful, and maybe even sophisticated men on their own ground in London they were prey to all kinds of dodgy characters. Lord Ogilvie allowed himself to be dragged into a card game where he was apparently so unlucky that not only did he lose all the cash he had, but was forced to hand over a bond to his ancestral lands in Angus! He then discovered the supposed gentlemen were card-sharpers and notorious cheats. When Donald heard of this he decided to do something about it. He went to the gambling-house where it had all happened and allowed himself to be persuaded by the same gamblers to play a hand or two of piquet. He had however taken the precaution of hiring a room and offered to play there. The three gamblers agreed, unaware that Ogilvie, Pitfoddels and friends were hiding in a small room next door. The game began, and even though one or other of the gamblers made a point of getting up every few minutes to fetch a drink or a titbit from the table behind Donald, he carefully kept his cards hidden. He also began upping the bets whenever he could, and the gamblers, thinking they had another dupe, went with him. Up and up the stakes rose till at last the gamblers were forced to bet the bond to Ogilvie's lands. Donald won again. By now the three gamblers were suspicious and looking around at last they noticed that there were cleverly angled mirrors above where they were sitting. Just as they were about to draw their swords, a door burst open and in rushed

Ogilvie and the others, swords in hand. The gamblers, realising they had been rumbled and unwilling to take on the Scots in a sword-fight, gave up and fled.

This story shows that Donald was a clever character, but he was most famous for another incident entirely.

Unknown to the Scots there was a famous Italian swordsman living in London at the time. He had challenged all and sundry amongst the 'cavaliers' of the town and had beaten every man who came against him. He considered himself the cock of the walk, and because he was undefeated he was effectively living off the people of London as he refused to pay for anything. In fact he had become so pompous that when he paraded around the city's streets he had a little Italian drummer-boy going before him beating his drum! The situation had become intolerable. One after another all the finest swordsmen of the time had gone against him. None escaped alive. The City of London burgesses even put up a reward for anyone who would beat this Italian upstart, but after a while there was no one who was prepared to face him. By this time even the king was keen to find a champion who would rid the city of the strutting Italian who regularly paraded up and down outside his palace with the drum pounding, declaiming that he would fight anybody anytime. The queen was also being driven distracted by this daily pantomime and asked around at court if there was no one in the entire kingdom who could rid them of this pest.

'Well, Your Majesty,' an old Lord said, 'there might be one. Donald Farquharson of Monaltrie, one of those wild Scots, is in town, and I have heard there is no better man with a sword in all Britain.'

The queen wasted no time in informing the king, who at once sent a messenger to fetch Donald. Donald was intrigued, a touch flattered to be summoned to meet the king and he hastened to the palace with the messenger. As they reached the palace, there was the Italian strutting up and down with his little drummer-boy pounding away. As Donald approached he whipped out his sword and stuck it through the drum.

'There now, that's enough of your din,' he said, and sheathed his sword and at once the Italian champion moved to block his way.

'And who are you, signor,' he hissed, 'that you value your life so cheaply?'

'I am Donald Farquharson of Monaltrie,' replied our hero, recognising the challenge, 'and I will gladly meet you at a place and time of your convenience.'

So the pleasantries preceding a duel were exchanged and arrangements were made for them to meet the following day in the morning at a nearby park.

Donald then went to meet the king, who, on telling him the task he wanted him to take on was delighted to hear that Farquharson had already arranged to meet the Italian in combat the following day.

'You must be careful Farquharson,' said the king, 'he seems to have almost supernatural powers, and none of our very finest men have ever been able to even scratch him.'

Donald spent the rest of the afternoon at the court, where it is said that many of the English ladies were very taken with his handsome looks, and there he heard more about the dangerous Italian. He soon realised that there was more to this man than just the strutting buffoon he appeared to be.

So that evening, after excusing himself from the court, Donald disguised himself as a manservant and made his way to where the Italian was lodging, free of course. Her made the acquaintance of the Italian's manservant and began to ply him with whisky, a drink the poor lad had never tasted before. He discovered quickly that he liked it, a lot. Soon in fact he was roarin' fou and began to spill the beans about his master's apparent invincibility. He had his arm round his new friend's shoulder and was slurring his words, but Donald soon got the gist of it.

'My master,' said the Italian, 'has a charmed life. No man born of woman can kill him, no man whose person bears iron can harm him; if you wear leather shoes you cannot touch him; no sword ever touched by iron or placed in a leather sheath can draw his blood, and even if a sword were found that could affect him, once it was withdrawn he would be made whole again. And as if that was not enough,' the Italian laughed, 'while he is fighting he has a shadow figure on either side so that it appears to his opponent as if there are three of him. He is invincible, but I hope he will take me home soon. Can I have some more of that whisky my friend?' And so saying he held up his glass which Donald was happy to refill. He knew now what he had to do and that he would have to be busy.

He had heard of a Moorish swordsmith in the city who made swords on a stone anvil with flint hammers and he had intended getting one of his blades anyway. He sent to have one of them delivered and stipulated that it must never have been in a leather sheath. He then found a tailor to make him a silken scabbard for the sword. Even in the middle of the night the tailor was happy to fulfil the commission given what Donald was prepared to pay. He also had a pair of silk shoes made overnight by a cobbler and in the morning he made sure that there was no piece of iron anywhere about his person before he strapped on his sword in its silk scabbard.

When he arrived at the designated place the Italian awaited him. On seeing that Donald had made careful preparations the Italian asked to see his sword. 'No, I think not,' replied Donald with a smile, and when the Italian reached out with his metal-tipped cane to try and touch the sword he simply moved back. 'Och, you will feel the touch of this sword soon enough,' he said.

The fight commenced and at once Donald saw three of the Italian before him. He simply concentrated on the one in the middle, and found he could parry his thrusts. He had heard that the Italian had a favourite trick where he leapt up high in the air and thrust down at his opponent. He was ready when this attack came and parried it with some ease. Again and again the Italian tried the move but every time the Scot parried him. This had been the trick that had carried the day for the Italian so often before. The sight of three men leaping down at them had obviously confused many swordsmen but Donald would not be fooled. He bided his time, and when the Italian leapt up again he lunged forward and stuck his sword through his opponent's ribs. At once he let go of the sword and the Italian fell to the ground.

'Ah, you have me,' cried the Italian. 'Pull your sword from my side and let me die in peace, Scotchman,' he pleaded.

'Och no, I think I will let the spit gang wi the roast,' replied the smiling Scot.

'The devil has kept ill faith with me,' screamed the Italian as he writhed in pain. 'No man of woman born should ever have overcome me.'

'Ah well,' replied Donald grimly, 'I never knew my mother, for she died in childbirth and I was cut from her side.'

The Italian looked at him in disbelief, gave a groan and died.

Now this you would think would have made our Donald a hero, but when later that day he was given the reward that had been put up by the City of London there was muttering in the watching crowd.

The comments were along the line of 'See how this Scotch beggar pockets our English gold,' and the usual 'This Scotch upstart is probably just like that Italian swine.'

Hearing this, Donald took the purse of gold he had been given, emptied the contents into his hand and scattered the whole lot among the watching crowd.

Turnig to Ogilvie and the others who had accompanied him he smiled and said, 'See how the English dogs gather up the gold they could not win themselves, but which a Scotsman won for them.'

No more was said. From then on he was given the name Domhull-og na-h-Alba, Young Donald of Scotland, and he said ever after that he was glad to return home, away from such a bunch of graceless ingrates.

Highland Candlesticks

There are many versions of this story, but this is most likely the oldest, if not the original one. Now the spelling of Gaelic names in both Scots and English was for long enough hardly an exact science, and that accounts for the various Mac, Mc and M' spellings that have survived to this day. Alexander MacDonnell was the tenth chief of his people, who lived around Keppoch in the shadow of Ben Nevis and spelt their name differently from the rest of the MacDonalds. Now by Alexander's time London was becoming an increasingly popular destination for clan chiefs. In earlier centuries, before the kingdoms of Scotland and England were united it had been quite normal for chiefs' sons to be educated on mainland Europe and many of them had travelled extensively. Now though, with the growth of the money economy and the weakening of the old blood ties of the clan system, many of the chiefs behaved little differently from the aristocratic classes of England and Lowland Scotland. London was the capital city where all power was concentrated and so very much 'the place to be' for those who considered themselves the natural leaders of society.

One time when Keppoch was in London he was invited to the home of an English aristocrat who was particularly proud of some silver candlesticks he had acquired. They had been imported from abroad, were very ornate and had cost the Englishman a great deal of money.

No doubt wishing to show his superiority over his northern companion he went on at length abut the quality and workmanship of the candlesticks and asked MacDonnell whether or not he had anything so fine back up in his mountains. Mac-Donnell looked at him for a few moments and said with a smile, 'I'll pay you three times their value if, when you come and visit me at Keppoch, you do not agree that I have candlesticks in my own home which are far better than these in both design and value.'

Now Highland chiefs were well known for their ostentation; it was a part of traditional clan behaviour that the clans took pride in the showiness of their chiefs, and the Englishman thought that the Scot was simply saying this out of a combination of clan and national pride. Sure that Keppoch could have nothing so fine at home in the semi-barbaric Highlands the aristocrat was more than happy to wager the price of the candlesticks against three times their value. When the Highlander then insisted that he come and visit him soon in his Highland home, the Englishman could hardly believe his luck. Like many of his sort he was intrigued by the idea of a visit to the wild Highlands, and the notion that he could make a substantial profit at the same time made this idea irresistible. Even though he quite liked this wild Highlander, who, truth to tell, was surprisingly sophisticated, he had no doubt that the bet was nothing more than Highland bravado!

So it was that a few months later the Englishman made his way up through England and Scotland to the MacDonnell's traditional clan lands of Keppoch. As he and his companions approached Keppoch's home on horseback, following half a dozen armed clansmen on foot, they were hardly impressed by Keppoch's home. True, it was two storeys high, and, unlike the vast majority of houses in the Highlands, had glass windows, but compared to the great classically influenced mansions that were all the rage amongst the English aristocracy of the time, it seemed to them rather pathetic. The Englishman who had taken the bet made a couple of remarks to his friends, certain that the Highlanders ahead of him wouldn't catch his meaning.

'Well. It is a fine house,' he smiled, 'to be up here in the Highlands, don't you think?'

'Oh yes, a fine dwelling indeed,' replied another with a smirk.

'And a magnificent setting,' added another, 'but perhaps a little wild for my taste.'

The MacDonnells who were acting as their guides, most of whom spoke English well, heard this and bit their tongues. Their ancestors would have responded to these insults with blows, but they restrained themselves, sure that MacDonnell himself would put these Southron mik-fed weaklings in their place. When they got to Keppoch House they were greeted by MacDonnell with a bumper of whisky and the English party were shown to their rooms, whose rather Spartan aspect merely reinforced the idea that the bet would be easily won.

A while later they were summoned to the dining hall of Keppoch House. As they came into the room, MacDonnell was sitting at the head of the table in the flickering light of fir torches. The chief silently motioned for them to take their seats. Then he smiled and waved his hand around the room. The Englishmen looked behind them. The light in the room was not much brighter than the candles they were used to, but they could clearly see that each of the six flaming torches was held high in the right hand of a powerfully built, bearded and fully armed Highlander!

'These,' said Keppoch, with a quiet smile, 'are my candlesticks and all the wealth of England could not buy even one of them.'

The English baron realised he had been thoroughly outfoxed and was happy to settle the debt and for the rest of his days he was happy to tell the story of the Chief's Candlesticks.

On the Battlefield

━━━◆◆◆◆━━━

In Roman Times

Some of the stories of the clans that have survived seem unlikely. One of these refers to an incident in Roman times around Lochearn. In those far-off days the clan system had yet to evolve, and the idea that there were two local tribes called MacLaren and MacCoul seems unlikely. However, there are also traditions in Perthshire that Pontius Pilate was born near Fortingall and that his mother was a MacKenzie. Precise historical accuracy has never been of importance in traditional storytelling and we should also remember that the tribes that lived in the Lochearn area two millennia ago were most likely the ancestors of the clans who eventually came into being there. It is also worth noting that we know that stories can carry accurate data over thousands of years, so maybe there is something to the tale!

Now the story goes that the Romans had set up their fort near Comrie, remnants of which can still be seen today. The Romans on building their fort had come to an arrangement with the chief of the local tribe, the MacLarens. Apart from agreeing to co-exist peacefully the MacLarens went further. The Roman soldiers, like their counterparts at all times all over the world tended to be fed a pretty boring diet. The necessity of supplying troops on campaign had led to a marvellous logistical catering process. No Roman soldier would ever go hungry, but whether they liked what they got is another matter. Around every fort they ever raised the Romans were used to merchants arranging the supply of local fresh produce to lighten up the dreary staple food of the camp. Often enough such merchants were Roman citizens themselves, who had come along with the campaign to try and make a living. The Roman commander had managed to get MacLaren to agree that a group of these traders would be allowed to go around the area buying up fresh produce like chickens, eggs and butter. These foodstuffs were guaranteed to make the merchants a fair profit as the soldiers were always clamouring for good fresh food. Now local tradition says that MacLaren was charging the Romans 'Black Mail' to protect them. As late as the eighteenth century landowners in Perthshire and Stirlingshire were entering into contracts of Blackmail with various Highland chieftains, effectively hiring them to keep other Highland raiders away from their property and their stock. As there are actual extant contracts of Blackmail the idea that it was no more than a protection racket has to be reconsidered and there are those that see it as an early form of insurance. Mind you there are still some today that see insurance as some form of racket too!

Anyway, while the Roman merchants were out in the glens around Lochearn trading for foodstuffs they were effectively under the direct protection of the Maclaren himself, and consequently of the whole clan. They therefore assumed that they did not require a military escort, and they saw no need to carry weapons themselves. However, there were always other clans roaming about the Highlands. One day the merchants were heading towards Comrie from St Fillans, totally unaware that they were being watched by a group of warriors on the slopes of Craig Liath to the north of Dunira. This was Finn MacCoul and his men who feature in so many ancient tales and legends. Maybe they had been having no luck in the hunt or perhaps their store of food was low. Whatever the reason, they saw the baskets of the Romans full of eggs and butter, cheese, bread and chickens and decided that they were in need of a feed. The first thing the Romans knew was when a large group of wild Highland warriors came charging down the hillside at them. They didn't hesitate, but fled the scene immediately, leaving Finn and his men to go off with the ponies without a fight. This they found very amusing.

The MacLaren however, was not amused when a group of exhausted Roman merchants arrived at his home at Tynreoch having run flat-out the two miles from where they had been attacked. They complained that he was supposed to protect them and here they had been robbed of all their goods barely two miles from his own home! This was a real insult, and MacLaren was furious and called for a party of warriors to be assembled right away. He would show these thieving MacCouls they couldn't get away with making a fool of him and the rest of the MacLarens. Just at that point a clansman arrived to say that he had seen a band of warriors heading through the hills by Loch Boltachan towards to Glen Tarken with a string of laden ponies.

It was only a matter of minutes before a strong band of warriors gathered in front of the chief's house and set off at a steady run towards the hills on the north side of Lochearn. Now up ahead of them the MacCouls were having trouble with one of the ponies which was a well-known stubborn brute. Having to keep 'geeing' this recalcitrant beast on every time it stopped, which was often, was really slowing the MacCouls down. So it was only a matter of time before the pursuing MacLarens caught up with them, on the flat lands lying at the feet of Meall nan Fiodh and Meall Reamhar.

The MacLarens were in no mood for parley. The MacCouls had insulted them before the visiting Romans and they were set on having their revenge. In the first rush several of the MacCouls went down and it was soon obvious that they were not just outnumbered but were also being out-fought. Realising that things were swinging against him and that more fighting could only lead to more losses, Finn called for his men to retreat and they fled the battle-scene, heading more deeply into the hills to the north. Their ill-gotten goods were left behind them to be returned to the Roman merchants. Having got the ponies back and sent several of the raiders to meet their ancestors was enough for the MacLaren to reckon that honour had been satisfied, but such was his pleasure at the outcome that he named the stream that flowed by where the battle was fought Allt-an-Fionn, the burn of Finn, and it carries that name to this day.

The Battle of the North Inch

One of the most famous of the clan battles was fought in 1396 on the Inch at Perth. The early Scottish historian Hector Boece says it was fought between the Clan Chattan and the Clan Cai. Nowadays we look on Clan Chattan as a confederation of clans from Strathspey and the surrounding districts, but it seems likely that here the reference is to the hereditary leaders of Clan Chattan, the MacPhersons. Their opponents on this occasion were the Clan Cai, more properly Clan Dhai, the Davidsons, who were themselves one of the component clans of the Clan Chattan confederation. It has been noted on many occasions down the years that if they had nobody else to fight, the Highlanders would fight each other. This statement, while a gross simplification, has a grain of truth. Because all men were warriors, and permanently 'on their honour' there were always plenty of reasons to pick a fight, if one was wanted, and clans who were sometimes at peace with one another, at other times could take great pleasure in raiding each other's cattle, with consequent battles thrown in. The cause of this particular struggle at Perth lay in an earlier fight – the Battle of Invernahaven. This had taken place ten years earlier, when the protagonists had been allied against the Camerons, and had resulted in a quarrel about who had the right to lead on the right side of the battle line. Such niceties may seem strange to the modern eye but in the days of the clan warriors, honour was a precise, precious and often dangerous concept. As a result of the falling-out the MacPhersons withdrew from that battle, leaving the Davidsons heavily outnumbered by the Camerons and conse-quently suffering a heavy defeat. This led to an ongoing feud and the Battle of North Inch was an attempt to settle the matter once and for all.

The king, Robert III, had tried to intercede to stop the feud, but to no avail. The upshot of this attempt however, was a suggestion from some of his noblemen that a battle could be fought to decide the matter for all time. Thirty men had been chosen to fight on behalf of each clan. This type of structured, almost ritual approach to battle was in fact common in warrior societies throughout Eurasia in earlier times and is a good illustration of the truly ancient aspect of much of Highland clan society – something that lasted for several centuries more. Sometimes champions were chosen to represent their peoples or tribes, David and Goliath being a weel-kent example. On other occasions, as at the Battle of the North Inch, a specified number of warriors would fight. Robert III probably saw an advantage in that the leading warriors of two of the most troublesome clans in the country would probably be killed in the battle – something that could only increase the chances of a more peaceful reign. Like most Scottish kings the problem of the perpetual raiding and battles in the Highlands caused him a great deal of trouble. Once the date for battle was set for 23 October the event began to take on something of the nature of a social occasion and many of the leading nobles and chiefs of Scotland were present with their ladies at the fateful encounter. They sat in specially built grandstands while the general popu-lace packed the sidelines behind barriers designed to keep them off the field of battle.

When all was set the combatants arrived, each group of clansmen preceded by their pipers. All were heavily armed with swords and targes, battle-axes and even bows and arrows. Then an odd thing happened. One of the MacPhersons, seeing the opposition and deciding he didn't fancy the idea of battle that day, ran off, jumped into the River Tay and swam across to the opposite bank. Behind him were the crowd of spectators, composed of many nobles and their families, while most of the population of Perth jeered and mocked the disappearing warrior. They had turned out in their thousands, hoping for a good entertainment! He also left behind him a bunch of infuriated kinsmen who were now one man short for the battle.

Furious discussion broke out, with both the Davidsons and the MacPhersons pleading with the king. The Davidsons wanted to proceed; after all, both sides had turned up with the right number of men and it was hardly their fault that one of the MacPhersons had shown himself to be such a coward. The MacPhersons for their part claimed that it was supposed to be a fair fight and that one of the Davidsons should withdraw to make the numbers even. Neither of them was prepared to give way and matters seemed to have reached an impasse when a local man intervened. This was Henry o' the Wynd, a Perth man of small and rather twisted stature who was both a smith and an armourer. Others say that he actually had the name Gow, or Smith, but there is little doubt that apart from being a reputable maker of weapons he also had the reputation of being extremely adept in their use.

He leapt the barrier, keeping the crowds back from the battleground, and walked straight up to where the leaders of the two clans were discussing matters with the king. Now this was hardly remarkable, as throughout medieval Scottish history even ordinary people were able to approach their monarchs in a direct way that would have been impossible in other, truly feudal contemporary societies like England or France. After all, Robert

III, like his predecessors, was King of Scots, not Scotland, a distinction that seemed to have had considerable significance in those far-off times. Gow walked up and spoke. 'I will gladly take part for an agreed fee – for the small price of half a mark – on one condition. If I survive this day I want to be kept by one of you, whoever wins, for the rest of my life.'

At first the combatants looked askance at this wee, twisted creature but once they were informed of his reputation as a man-at-arms, they saw the sense in his proposal. This was an offer that would allow matters to proceed, so the chiefs of the respective clans agreed that Henry o' the Wynd, An Gobha Crom, the Crooked Smith, would fight on the side of the MacPhersons. As soon as this was announced to the crowd, cheering broke out amongst the nobles and their ladies and the common people who had gathered in their thousands to see this combat. Now the entertainment could start and there would be blood spilt!

The battle was signalled to begin, and true to his hire Gow quickly loosed off an arrow which felled one of the Davidsons. All the others on both sides loosed their arrows, and throwing down their bows they ran towards each other, screaming their battle slogans, and hand-to-hand fighting began. Gow, though, stood where he was. The leader of the MacPhersons, Sgorr-fiachlach or Buck-toothed Shaw, noticed this, and before running to close with the enemy asked him, 'What are you doing man?'

'I have earned my fee I think, I have killed my man,' the smith calmly replied.

The MacPherson was a true leader of men and swiftly came back at him: 'The man who keeps no reckoning of his good deeds, without reckoning shall be repaid.'

This was good enough for Henry and the pair of them ran into the surging battle. Now in those days of hand-to-hand combat with sword and targe, or battle-axe and broadsword, things were bloody indeed, particularly as all present were intent on fighting to victory or death. There is no need here to go into the gory details of split skulls and severed limbs. Suffice it to say that the bloodthirsty crowd were in no way disappointed. As the battle raged the advantage began to go in favour of the MacPhersons. This was greatly helped by the skill and dexterity of the crooked smith whose strength and agility were remarkable. After a considerable time the MacPhersons were eventually declared the winners. And rightly so. For though the eleven survivors were all badly wounded, with the notable exception of the Perth smith, only one of the Davidson contingent was still breathing.

Henry o' the Wynd, the Gow Crom was adopted into the MacPherson clan after his magnificent display of fighting skills that day on the North Inch and he was given lands by the chief. It is from him that the Gow sept of that clan claim their descent. As to Robert III's fervent hope for peace in the Highlands, well things were quiet in Badenoch and Strathspey after the Battle of the North Inch, but only for a little while.

The Battle of Harlaw

One of the finest and best-known ballads still sung in Scotland is 'The Battle of Harlaw'. In the ballad, the story is given that a force of Highlanders, under the leadership of the MacDonald, is coming through Morayshire till they meet with a group of local lairds led by James the Rose and John the Graham. While the ballad presents the battle as essentially a great fight between Highlanders and Lowlanders the truth is slightly different. But then again the purpose of the ballads was as much to entertain as to inform. Like the telling of traditional stories the importance of the ballads was to tell a good story, perhaps underline a moral point, but the idea of strict historical accuracy had no place. The ballad reflects the hold that the battle had on the public imagination, for it is said that Harlaw was played out by boys throughout Scotland for more than a hundred years after the battle itself.

In 1411 Donald, Lord of the Isles, had his ambitions on the mainland thwarted. He had married Margaret, a granddaughter of the last Earl of Ross. The earl had left no male heir and the inheritance passed to the distaff side. His daughter had had two children, Margaret and her brother Alexander. Alexander had also died, and was survived by his daughter Euphemia. Euphemia was not a worldly lass and she decided she wanted to become a nun, and on so doing she resigned her right in the Earldom of Ross to her uncle John Stewart, the Earl of Buchan. Donald claimed she had no right to do this and that the title should revert to his wife and thus to him. Now the Duke of Albany, Governor of Scotland, had been instrumental in getting Euphemia to give up her title to her uncle and was in no way prepared to allow the Lord of the Isles to take over the great lands of Ross-shire. Donald was already too powerful, according to the establishment powers in Edinburgh. He was also secretly allied with the King of England, who supplied him with a good number of ships, allowing him to lead a force of MacDonalds and several thousand other clansmen from the west into Ross. They laid waste much of the country before meeting strong resistance in a battle near Dingwall. The opposing forces were led by Angus Dubh, Black Angus, Mackay and his brother Roderick. The two armies clashed, and the Islesmen were tepmporarily halted – but at the cost of the lives of Angus, Roderick and a great many of their men.

This only made Donald keener than ever to ransack as much of the mainland as he could. Now at various times in his ongoing battles with mainlanders he had expressed the wish to burn Aberdeen. This was the furthest north of any sizeable town, and Donald saw it as representative of all that he hated about the centralising powers of the Scottish kings and their supporters in Edinburgh. The fact that it was also a prosperous place with many well-off merchants might have helped make it a pretty attractive target as well.

So once his men had recovered from the battle at Dingwall he decided that he would go straight to Aberdeen and show the townspeople just who was boss of northern Scotland. Stopping at Inverness to summon more clansmen loyal to his cause – or more truly to the cause of plunder – he then set off through the fertile lands of Moray, his army taking anything and everything they could find in the way of goods and gear and cattle. They came as far as Strathbogie, despoiling the entire countryside as they passed.

By this time the inhabitants of Aberdeen were well aware of the approaching storm and were in a panic. The Earl of Mar, Duncan Stewart, was a son of one of the greatest of the Highland raiders, the Wolf of Badenoch. He was by now an experienced soldier himself and was ready to take on the rampaging Islesmen. He had a much smaller force consisting of his own Stewart clansmen and contingents of Forbeses, Keiths and Leslies from Aberdeenshire and others from further south. Most of these however were well-mounted men, with up-to-date armour, while the majority of the clansmen possessed swords, spears and targes, and the odd hauberk of chain mail or leather. Though they were better armed and a few of them were Scots speakers, most were either Gaelic-speakers or were bilingual. The popular idea that this was a battle between Highlander and Lowlander, Gael and Scot, is a bit too simplistic. The motive behind the battle was Donald's desire to get the Earldom of Ross for himself. He probably thought that if he raided the North-east in sufficient force then Albany, the Governor, would accede to his claim. His followers of course were mainly in it for the raiding, just as their ancestors, the Vikings, Scots and Picts had been so many centuries earlier.

Mar's force also had representatives of many notable Lowland families, Ogilvies from Angus, Scrymgeours from Dundee,

Murrays, Irvings and Leslies, as well as Robert Davidson, the Provost of Aberdeen, and a group of the town's armed inhabitants. Heading north-west from Aberdeen, Mar led his force up the Don water to Inverurie. Just up the Ury water at Harlaw the Islesmen had stopped. It was obvious to Mar and his companions that they were heavily outnumbered and even with the advantage of armoured cavalry they realised his chances of victory weren't that good. Because the mail-clad horsemen had been trained to fight in groups, while the MacDonalds and their allies would rely on the impetus of the charge and the traditional skills with axe and sword at close quarters, Mar considered that the battle was worth the risk.

So began a bloody day's work. The Highlanders, the vast majority on foot, were no match one-on-one for the armoured horsemen, but their numbers were considerable and their bravery never in doubt. The Highlanders charged furiously at the men-at-arms, and as their front lines fell before the lances of the horsemen others rushed to fill the gaps. Sir James Scrymgeour, the constable of Dundee, held his line firm then forced his contingent deep into the Highland forces. Hacking and chopping at the men surging around them, one after another they were pulled from their horses or had the great beasts hamstrung under them before falling below the dirks and swords of their assailants. Soon the entire Dundee contingent had disappeared. Elsewhere the other Lowland forces were surrounded in small groups. One by one the mounted men fell, their ranks closing more tightly against the constant surge of the enemy. No matter how many men fell before the horsemen, more kept coming. At last, as night fell the Highlanders fell back, letting Mar's exhausted troops retreat from the battlefield and rest. It was clear that no one had as yet gained a decisive advantage, but Mar and his men knew that they could not continue to sustain the rate of losses they had taken for another day. Things were still in the balance.

Then something happened that in the long-run saved every-body's face. A large group of the Islesmen had gone in at a wide arc in order to come up behind Mar, and they had come across the Lowlander's baggage train, containing weapons, food, horses and even spare chain-mail. Here was treasure indeed, a prize worth the fighting that had taken place this far. There was more than enough to go round so when they convoyed the baggage train back to the rest of their fellows, plenty of them had what they considered sufficient booty for their endeavours. So in the night much of the MacDonald force simply marched back home with their profits. This after all was what they went raiding for, and there were plenty of cattle that had been left behind by the main force to pick up as they went. All in all, for most of them it had resulted in a very profitable expedition. With so many of his men having decided to head home there was little point in Donald staying, so he went back with them. Most considered that they had won a great victory – well, look at what they were taking home with them! Later Donald would say that he had so whittled down Mar's men that there was no real reason for wiping them out. He had made his point and gone home!

Come the morning, Mar and his men, spared the horrors of another day of steady attrition, were more than happy to claim victory for their own side. After all, hadn't they seen off the threat to Aberdeen and sent the wild men of the Isles back home to think again? The wiser heads among them may have realised that they had had a lucky escape, but there was no way they wouldn't proclaim this as a great victory. So both sides won. But it was a sore win for Mar's men. Throughout Angus and the Mearns family after family had lost its head. Lesley of Balquhain is said to have fallen with six of his sons. Alongside Sir James Scrymgeour, Sir Alexander Ogilvy, the sheriff of Angus, his eldest son George Ogilvy, Sir Thomas Murray, Sir Robert Maule of Panmure, Sir Alexander Irving of Drum, Sir William Abernethy of Saltoun, Sir Alexander Straiton of Lauriston,

James Lovel and Alexander Stirling all lay on the battlefield. From Aberdeen, Sir Robert Davidson, the Provost, most of the principal gentry of Buchan, and the greater part of the burgesses of Aberdeen would never see home again. They might have had knightly titles from the King, and many of them spoke Scots as their first tongue, but they were in truth little different from the chiefs of the Highland clans who also had laid down their lives that day.

The ballad talks of 40,000 Highlandmen, but in truth the numbers were never that large. Donald's forces perhaps were as much as 8,000, while the brave Lowland force was less than 1,500, which even with the advantages of horses and armour showed great courage. Donald is thought to have lost about 900 men on the battlefield while his enemies lost much fewer, about 500; but this was over a third of their total. The battle was caused by Donald's attempts to get the Earldom of Ross and the struggle went on for a few years more before he finally gave up. But the epic struggle of that day lives on in song and for many years was presented as a showdown between Gaelic and Scots speakers.

In reality, on that July day in 1411 it was just another battle, if a major one, between Highland clans and Lowland families, the like of which continued for centuries to come

The Battle of the Park

At one time the chief of the MacDonalds was more than just the hereditary leader of the biggest clan of all. In the early Middle Ages the MacDonald chiefs held the title of Lord of the Isles. Their control over the Hebrides effectively made them a separate country. In fact it was not unknown for the Lord of the Isles to enter into alliances with the King of England against the King of Scotland, if he thought it to his or his people's advantage. The MacDonalds, like all other clans, saw loyalty to their kin and control of their own lands as the most important aspects of their social existence, and the idea of Scotland as a nation was not one they really subscribed to. The growth of the Lordship of the Isles had come about through a combination of the native Gaelic-speaking tribes with incoming groups of Germanic-speaking Norsemen, who initially came raiding as the Vikings but soon began to settle in many parts of Western Scotland and Ireland. Several Highland clans trace their origins back to noted Norse leaders. The Lords of the Isles had one particular advantage. Their main means of communication, because of the scattered islands that they controlled, was the sea. Sea communication, particularly in times of good weather, was much more efficient than overland travel in the days when much of Scotland was still heavily forested and a great deal of the remainder was boggy ground. It wasn't until the so-called 'improvements' in agriculture from the seventeenth century onwards, that large parts of Scotland were drained, leading to the Lowland landscape we know today. Sea travel on board the birlinns, the traditional galleys of the Western Isles, meant that the Lords of the Isles had quick and efficient communications throughout most of their possessions. However king-like the Lords of the Isle may have thought themselves, other clan chiefs considered the MacDonalds to be no more important than their own kin and were often ready to take them on in battle. One such battle was Blar-na-pairc, fought at Kinellan in 1488.

Like many other clans the MacDonalds would often try to establish alliances with other clans through marriage, and when Alexander, chief of the MacKenzies, suggested that Margaret, the daughter of John, Lord of the Isles, should marry his son Kenneth MacKenzie, John was happy to accept. Alexander was getting on in years at the time and wished to leave his son as chief in a position where the traditional battles with the MacDonalds were a thing of the past. So the marriage went ahead and at first all seemed to go well.

It so happened that in the year following the marriage, John's nephew Alexander MacDonald of Keppoch, who was in line to become Lord of the Isles himself, had taken over some lands at Balcony in Ross-shire. The marriage of his cousin Margaret to the son of the chief of the MacKenzies had made this seem less dangerous than it might have been before the marriage. Now one of the marks of chiefly behaviour amongst the Highland clans was ostentation. Chiefs liked to show off their wealth by throwing great feasts and being generous, and this was supported by their kinfolk, the everyday members of the clan. In fact it was a matter of honour for the Highland warriors that their chiefs had to look good and be generous even if the rest of the clan might appear to be poverty-stricken. After all, on a fundamental level the office of chief, not the person, was the embodiment of the whole clan, and fights often broke out about precedence when warriors from one clan thought their chief was not being given due honour. To say that the average Highland warrior was a bit prickly in matters of honour is a severe understatement of the facts, and of course the chiefs themselves were often even worse. What appear to us to be trivial slights could lead to extensive loss of life.

Alexander MacDonald, as the putative heir to the Lordship of the Isles and effectively to the most important chiefship of them all, was no different from the rest of his contemporaries. The Christmas following his settling in Ross he decided to hold a feast. He therefore organised all the necessary drinks and food and invited all of the leading chiefs of the area to join him. It was to be a great show of ostentation. However, there was one problem. He had only recently taken over Balcony and though the big house was a fine building for its time many of the other buildings around it were rather crude, and accommodation for his guests was a bit scarcer than some of them might have expected. Now Kenneth MacKenzie, being married to Alexander's cousin, was to be an honoured guest, but for some reason Kenneth did not arrive till Christmas Eve, accompanied by forty of his MacKenzie kin, all of them warriors, which was quite normal. However, there was no sign of Margaret and Alexander was affronted at the absence of his cousin from such a great social affair. Things got worse, quickly.

Alexander had given MacLean of Duart the job of organising the accommodation for his guests. Now Kenneth and MacLean had had words not long before at one of the sporting gatherings beloved of the Highlanders, and though it had not led to blows at the time, there was ill-will between them. According to MacLean the reasons for the dispute were the shortage of places, the lateness of the hour and the necessity for Kenneth and his men to sleep in the corn-drying kiln, basically a simple wooden barn some distance from the main house. The son of the chief of the MacKenzies being put up in a kiln! There was no way Kenneth would tolerate this, and he punched Maclean on the ear, knocking him to the ground. The MacDonalds who were around immediately drew their weapons at this insult and Kenneth realised that he was in deep water; his forty warriors were overwhelmingly outnumbered by the MacDonalds and their allies, many of whom had already come to Balcony for the feast.

Looking around he noticed that there were a fair number of birlinns drawn up on the shore.

'To the boats, lads,' he shouted and ran to the beach. Stopping only to bash holes in as many boats as they could the forty MacKenzies got into four vessels and made for the opposite shore. They had acted just quickly enough to make their escape. Once they had landed on the other side of the sea loch they found shelter with a local man who so impressed Kenneth that he asked him if he wanted to become a MacKenzie. Now this was something that sometimes happened amongst the clans. Sometimes families could be thrown out by their own kin and would accept the leadership of another chief, taking the clan name as a mark of respect. Now his host was prepared to accept what he saw as an honour, and though we do not know what, if any clan he came from it is pretty clear that he probably wasn't a MacDonald! Now Kenneth was deeply upset at what he saw as the insult given him by MacLean and reckoned that it was down to Alexander MacDonald himself: after all, MacLean had merely been doing his bidding. As was so often the case, once a Highlander thought he had been insulted, things rapidly worsened.

His first move the next day, Christmas, was to go to nearby Chanonry and call on the bishop there to come and meet him. The bishop knew Kenneth (and his reputation), so he decided that despite the day it would be politic to see what the MacKenzie heir wanted. Back in those times much of the land of Scotland was in church ownership and the bishop was relieved to find out that Kenneth was simply requesting him to draw up a charter for the tenancy of the land on which Kenneth and his men had found hospitality the night before. This would effectively put this bit of land under MacKenzie control and would cement his new relationship with the previous night's host. It also would allow him to let MacDonald know that he had spent Christmas on his own land rather than on some stranger's. The bishop then instructed a clerk to draw up the necessary let of the clachan or township of Cullicudden in Kenneth's name. Such were the niceties of Highland honour in those distant times. But Kenneth was not finished. He returned the next day to join his father at Kinellan, not far from the modern town of Strathpeffer.

The old man was hardly pleased with his headstrong son. He had been trying to avoid further troubles with the powerful MacDonalds and here Kenneth had apparently started a brand new feud. Although there were not very many MacDonalds in Rossshire at the time, they could call on considerable numbers of their kin from other parts of the country. The MacKenzies were outmatched according to Alisdair.

'A McKenzie is worth ten MacDonalds any day,' came the angry retort from Kenneth when the realities of the situation were pointed out to him. 'I will not stand still for the insult they have given us,' he fumed.

He wasn't the only one fuming. Only a few days later an ominous letter arrived from MacDonald. Claiming the rights of his uncle, as Earl of Ross, he demanded that Kenneth, his father and all the MacKenzies depart form Kinellan at once, giving leave for his cousin Margaret to take her own time to follow the MacKenzies. If his commands were not obeyed, the messenger told the MacKenzies, MacDonald would enforce his orders, promising war to the knife, a clear statement of intent.

If Kenneth had been angry before he was now incandescent with fury. He was the wronged party as he saw it, and here was this upstart MacDonald acting as if he was his lord and master. He sent a message back to MacDonald telling him that both he and his father had no intention of moving and that he (Mac-Donald) could try his worst. But, true to his own character Kenneth could hardly leave it at that and added a postscript saying that as there would now be no peace between the MacKenzies and the MacDonalds he was returning his wife to her own kin, thereby ending the marriage. Now this was a further insult that could only stoke things up, but Kenneth was not finished. Although they had not yet been married for two years, it would appear as if he were tiring of his bride already, despite the fact that she had already borne him a son, also called Kenneth. It was an unfortunate fact that due to a childhood accident Margaret was blind in one eye.

Kenneth had her sent to Alexander at Balcony House, mounted on a one-eyed horse, accompanied by a one-eyed servant and followed by a dog that was also one-eyed. This was a grievous insult to Lady Margaret and all her kin. There was no way that battle could now be avoided and every action was guaranteed to increase the certainty of more bloodshed.

Kenneth, by now showing his true colours, had gone ahead with all of this without consulting his father who, as hereditary chief of the MacKenzies, was supposed to be in overall charge of the clan. Kenneth's rage, however, led him to ignore all the proprieties of normal behaviour. Within days of throwing Margaret out he laid siege to Lovat, chief of the Frasers, in order to demand his daughter Agnes as his next wife! He was certainly a man who knew what he wanted and was determined to get it. In his inimitable style he promised Lovat bonds of friendship if he agreed, but declared he would be his lifelong enemy if he refused. Diplomacy was not an attribute that could be associated with Kenneth at this stage. Having said that though, Kenneth was no fool and was well aware that Lovat, like many of the chiefs of the clans in north and western Scotland, was extremely suspicious of the power of the MacDonalds and resented the position of the Lord of the Isles. So Lovat sent word to the large force of Mackenzies, over 200 of them, camped at his door, that if Agnes would have Kenneth he had no objection to the marriage. Agnes agreed, and forthwith set out with Kenneth to Kinellan. There is no record of any clergy being involved, but as ever in the Highlands necessity proved more important than the niceties of religion.

By now battle was inevitable. There was no way either side could back down in the light of the various insults that had flown back and forth. Alexander sent MacLean off to tour round the islands to raise men for an attack on the MacKenzies. Word was also sent to other groups of MacDonalds in Ardnamurchan and Moidart. Before long significant numbers had rallied to Alexander – estimates range from about 1,500 to 3,000 men – a substantial number of warriors for any Highland battle. The situation was complicated by national politics. The ongoing power-struggle between the monarch, James III, and the Lord of the Isles meant that it was not a good time for the MacDonalds to carry out a major incursion on the MacKenzies, whether in their traditional homelands of Kintail or at Kinellan in Easter Ross. But Kenneth had plans of his own. He advanced to Kintail where he provisioned the castle of Eilean Donnan for a long siege, dispersing the cattle and other moveable goods of his clan among the hills. He then returned to Kinellan with MacKenzies from a variety of locations. They all knew that they were potentially so outnumbered as to make a pitched battle almost a foregone conclusion – a MacDonald victory – but they were all determined to defend the honour of their leaders and their kin.

Meanwhile Alexander was also on the move. He led his substantial army through the lands of Lochaber and Badenoch and up towards Inverness. On the way they were joined by some men from Clan Chattan. They took time to lay siege to Lovat's Castle at Kilravock, which they demolished before heading north. Soon they were in the lands of Strathconan, MacKenzie territory, where they killed all the close relatives of Kenneth that they found. Now the bloodthirstiness of Highland raids and battles has long been over-stated but there were times when the behaviour of Highland warriors was utterly despicable.

Alexander was determined to make the MacKenzies pay for the insults he had received at Kenneth's hands and when he and his men arrived at Contin by the River Conan a truly dreadful deed took place. Hearing of the approach of the men from the west the local population, mostly women and children and old men incapable of wielding a weapon, had all gathered in the church. The able-bodied men had already left to join the clan force at Kinellan. The remaining MacKenzies put their faith in the power of religion to defend them from the revenge of the MacDonalds. After all, they were no threat whatsoever to Alexander.

But Alexander was hell-bent on revenge, and, realising that the church was jam-packed full of MacKenzies, he had the doors barred from the outside and set fire to the church. The old, the children and the women-folk perished horrendously in the flames along with the priest. If Alexander had any religious feelings they certainly were no match for his lust for vengeance on Kenneth. The fighting men of the MacKenzies were only a few miles north when this dreadful event took place and word soon reached them from some of the people who had *not* taken refuge in the church when the MacDonalds arrived.

The anger of the MacKenzies can be imagined when so many of them heard what had happened to their wives, children and parents. Kenneth was now incandescent and informed his men that the actions of the MacDonalds had put them beyond the pale and that effectively they now had God on their side; such was the blasphemous action of the men from the west. Unscrupulous politicians and warmongers have often used this as an excuse, but in this case Kenneth surely had some justification. Now Alexander MacDonald knew that he had at least three times as many men as Kenneth had, and he was pretty sure that he would not want to face him in open battle. However, he forgot that they were on ground that Kenneth knew well. He had deployed his men in a hilltop position which they could defend against superior numbers. He also realised that with such a large body of troops Alexander would have trouble even feeding them. Most of the cattle and much of the grain in the area had already been moved out of harm's way and Kenneth himself had plenty of provisions for his own men. Contingency plans had also been made for a retreat, if necessary, to the height of Raven's Rock overlooking Strathpeffer where the old chief and a select band of warriors had already gone. This was an almost impregnable position. In the end this foresight was irrelevant; things were settled on the field of battle.

The rest of the MacDonalds were drawn up on a large boggy area of ground like a big field or park, called *pairc* in Gaelic.

Now Kenneth was on home ground, and seeing how the MacDonalds had organised their forces he came up with a daring plan. He sent his younger brother off with a bunch of

62

capable bowmen to the side of the boggy area to lie in ambush He then advanced to meet the enemy with the intention of retreating and drawing the MacDonalds on to the arrows of Duncan's contingent. Once Donald's men were in position he advanced, the MacKenzies being accompanied by the chief of the Brodie clan who had dropped in on Kenneth the day before on his way to collect cattle on the west coast, and a band of his men.

At the head of the opposing forces Alexander MacDonald turned to the most experienced of the clan's warriors, a grizzled veteran by the name of Gillespic, and said, 'That fool Mackenzie is playing right into our hands with this madness. Attacking a force three times as big as his own head on, is the act of a desperate and foolish man. Let's be at him.'

'I suggest caution here,' the older man said, 'this apparent madness might not be what it seems. It's always a good idea to treat extraordinary boldness with extreme wariness in my experience.'

This infuriated Alexander: 'If that's how you feel old man, why don't you go and fight alongside MacKenzie? It will make no difference to the outcome. You will both just be a breakfast to me and mine.'

This was a dreadful insult to the older man who had been loyal to his kin in battle after battle throughout his life. But although Alexander was every bit as headstrong and impetuous as Kenneth MacKenzie, he was not as smart. Gillespie, smitten by this grievous insult, bit his tongue. Alexander was the heir to the chief, and he might be a bumptious young oaf, but there was work to be done for the MacDonalds that day – hard and bloody work despite what the young fool had to say.

As Kenneth advanced with his clan the vanguard of the MacDonalds came straight at them. They were being led by MacLean of Lochbuie. The two sides clashed and for a while the fighting was fierce, with men falling on both sides.

Then the MacKenzies began to retreat. But they were retreating through moss and bog which they. It was new ground to the MacDonalds and their allies. Soon they were literally getting bogged down and were almost at a standstill. At this point a rank-thinning shower-hail of arrows fell amongst them and Duncan charged their flank and rear with his small contingent. Their surprise assault was deadly and the carnage amongst the MacDonalds was significant. Those who did not fall in the vicious attack turned and ran back towards their own main force. Duncan didn't hesitate but pursued them at full tilt, with Kenneth and the rest of the MacKenzies coming as fast as they could to catch them up.

The retreating MacDonalds and MacLeans got tangled up in the front lines of their main force and before they could organise themselves the Mackenzies were on them, driving them back. Gilespic, cursing Alexander's stupidity under his breath, decided there was only one way to turn the tide. The impetus of the Mackenzies was causing widespread confusion and despite the superior MacDonald numbers he knew the day was in the balance. He resolved to find and kill Kenneth. That would probably halt the Mackenzies and he and his kin would be able to regroup.

Kenneth realised what was happening, and understanding what the older warrior intended, he headed towards him. Both men lost the lives of several of their foes as they fought to meet each other. It was to be a one-to-one fight and one which could easily decide the eventual outcome of the bloody carnage taking place all across the park. Now Gillespic was a well-seasoned warrior and a man whose bravery, despite Alexander's insult, was well known, but Kenneth had the strength of youth on his side and when they met it didn't take long. After exchanging no more than a few strikes with their great double-handed broadswords Kenneth saw his chance and dealt Gillespic a mighty blow, severing his arm and killing him outright.

The story then goes that Kenneth looked round and saw the MacKenzie standard-bearer fighting near him.

He felled his man, and as a break came in the fighting directly around them Kenneth shouted at him, 'Where is our standard? Have you abandoned your post man?'

'Och no, I would not do such a thing,' came the reply, 'I have left our standard in the care of the MacDonald's standard-bearer, and he is looking after it with no thought of his own chief or kin.'

'What is the meaning of that?' demanded the puzzled Kenneth. 'Well,' answered the man, 'we met, and I had the best of it, and seeing there is much work to do and there are so many more of them I simply stuck our flag into his body and got to work. I left a couple of lads to look after it in case of trouble, but they won't be troubled much I am thinking. Look over there.'

Kenneth looked where he pointed, and sure enough, he could make out the MacKenzie flag flying, now a fair bit behind where they now stood. Such had been the effect of Duncan's actions and the turmoil in the MacDonald ranks that they could not manage to rally and many of them were cut down as they fled the field. The MacKenzies were triumphant and such was the contribution of the Brodies that day – their young chief was sorely injured but he recovered in time – that a bond of friendship was established which lasted for centuries. It was a famous victory and has gone down in the annals as *Blar-na-Pairc*, the Battle of the Park. Tradition tells us that such was the extent of the victory that day that some of the MacKenzies were successful in capturing Alexander MacDonald himself.

The fleeing MacDonalds were chased south to prevent any possibility of them rallying and coming to rescue their leader, and in this the MacKenzies had the help of a group of Frasers, relatives of Kenneth's new wife Agnes. They were led by one of their smiths – a profession that included many mighty warriors throughout Scotland's turbulent history – who had arrived too late for the battle itself but were leased to assist in the mopping-up afterwards. The nature of Highland warfare, and the raiding which led to so much of it was such that there is little wonder that a few old scores were paid off as the MacKenzies chased the remnants of the MacDonald force south. The Munros, some of whom had accompanied the MacDonalds on the way to Kinellan and in the battle itself were particularly hard hit, and despite the weakening of the MacDonalds, who soon after this lost the Lordship of the Isles, the king's representative in the North, the Earl of Huntly, was forced to rein in the MacKenzies.

And as for Alexander MacDonald of Lochalsh, he could not really have expected much other than a swift death after the burning at Contin but Kenneth surprised him and many others by his subsequent actions. When he and his old father met up again at Kinellan after it was all over, Alisdair told his son that capturing Alexander was perhaps not the best thing to do. Sparing his life, he suggested, just made it all the more likely that Alexander would be able to cause them trouble in the future. However, killing him in the heat of the battle and executing him once he had been made prisoner were two different things, and Kenneth treated his enemy with the respect and honour due to a fellow chief.

In fact after six months Kenneth went so far as to return Alexander to his own people, but the consequences of the battle were still unfolding. Not only did neither Alexander nor the Lord of the Isles seek revenge, they found it difficult to protect their own. Their strength was substantially diminished following the great losses in the north, and just a few years later, in 1493, the Scottish Parliament deemed that the possessions of the Lord of the Isles were forfeit to the Crown. The major raid that culminated in the Battle of the Park was merely the last of a series of events that saw the great power of the MacDonalds at last being diminished. By this time Kenneth had succeeded Alisdair as chief of the MacKenzie clan and had actually won favour with the king, James III, and his successor James IV.

After *Blar-na-pairc*, Kenneth was known as Kenneth of the Battles, which seems a fitting nickname for one so obviously headstrong and argumentative, though his own descendants will say that it was because of his significant victory over the MacDonalds that day. And from that time onwards Kenneth was in truth highly regarded amongst all the clans of the north for how he had turned the tables on the superior forces of the MacDonalds. He soon became known as a wise and just chief, respected by the people of his own clan and many others.

Big Duncan of the Axe

Shortly before the first blows at the famous Battle of the Park a big, young and kind of rough-looking lad, still in his teens, was seen wandering about near the gathered MacKenzies, as if he had lost something. Several of the clansmen noticed him, recognising he was a local lad called Duncan MacRae that some perhaps thought a little foolish. Whatever he was doing they paid little attention. They were concentrating on more pressing matters at hand – the imminent battle with the invading MacDonald forces. The main force had just headed towards the enemy lines when the young lad bent down in the heather with a grunt of satisfaction and came holding an old, rusted, but still sharp axe.

Carrying it over his shoulder he ran after the others, catching up with them just as battle commenced. However he just wandered up and down in a gormless fashion, looking at the fighting, then walking a bit more, stopping and taking another look, and so on. At one point he came near to Hector Roy, third son of Alisdair MacKenzie, the chief who was directing part of the battle. Seeing the lad, Hector called out to him: 'Whatever are you doing boy? Why are you not fighting alongside your kinsfolk?'

'Ah well,' shouted Duncan, 'If I do not get the esteem due to a man I will not do a man's work.'

This was a reference to the fact that, due to his odd ways he had not been given a weapon for the fight, though like all other Highland lads he had been trained in arms since childhood. Hector was a bit put out at this, and snapped at the lad, 'Do a man's work and you will get a man's esteem,' before returning to the fray.

At once Duncan leapt into the battle shouting. 'A heavy blow from the back of my hand. He who does not get out of my way, let me get out of his.'

He wielded the axe with great strength and skill and within a minute or two had killed one of the MacDonald forces. He pulled the body of his foe to one side of the fighting and sat on a nearby rock. Again Hector Roy noticed him and shouted at him, 'Why have you stopped now?'

'Well, if I only get one man's due I will only do one man's work.'

Hector, who was a bit busy himself, managed to call out that he would get two men's due if he did two men's work. He was probably thinking that this was taking the idea of one-on-one fighting a bit too literally, but he soon had to concentrate on his own prowess against the enemy. Duncan, hearing this, once again plunged into the battle.

Yet again he killed the first man he fought with, and yet again he dragged the body to one side of the conflict and sat down. Hector, who had despatched his own opponent by this time, again asked what he was doing and as before he got a similar reply.

'For God's sake laddie, just get to it and we will have no reckoning with you,' Hector said, clearly getting angry.

'He that would not reckon with me,' replied Duncan, realising by now that he had better do as he was told, 'I would not reckon with him.' And once more he went back to swinging his axe. The story goes that he entered into the thickest part of the fray and that the enemy fell like blades of grass before his whirling, rusty battle-axe. This was noticed by MacLean of Lochbuie, the leader of the vanguard of the MacDonald forces now struggling with the MacKenzies, and he resolved to sort out this young warrior once and for all. He forced his way through the battling warriors to come face to face with Duncan.

Now MacLean was a mighty warrior, and had fought in a hundred battles without suffering defeat. He also had the advantage of wearing chain-mail while Duncan had no armour of any kind, not even a helmet. The strength and skill of MacLean began to tell as he drove the young man backwards. Duncan though, with no armour, could move more quickly than his opponent and MacLean was unable to land a telling blow. Still he forced Duncan back. Back and back he went, taking every opportunity to glance quickly behind him till he was perched on the edge of a ditch. MacLean, thinking he now had Duncan at his mercy, swung a great blow with his sword. Duncan ducked the blow, at the same time leaping backwards across the ditch. MacLean's sword whistled through the air and squelched into the boggy peaty ground. Leaning forward to yank his sword free, MacLean's helmet rose from his neck, exposing a gap of no more than an inch. It was enough. Using all his agility Duncan leapt forward and brought his axe down on the gap between helmet and chain-mail. Such was the power of the stroke that MacLean's head flew from his body.

All the MacDonald fighters in the immediate area saw what had happened, and, already sorely pressed on two sides by Kenneth's and Duncan's contingents, they began to fall back. The loss of the leader of their vanguard was a devastating blow. He was a warrior famed throughout Scotland and the MacDonalds, already being forced back, began to run from their foes. It was this rout falling back on the front lines of the main Mac-Donald force that turned the battle. The retreating men caused confusion amongst their own lines and the MacKenzies soon had the upper hand.

Duncan may have been reluctant to start, but once he had started, he intended finishing, but even after his heroics thus far, he was not finished. Later that night, after the battle, while MacDonalds were still being hunted down, Kenneth was sitting by the fire at Kinellan when he heard the story of Big Duncan's exploits. He was impressed. 'And where is he now, this fine young warrior?' he asked the men around him. 'Well, the last I saw of him,' said one of the MacRaes who was there, 'he was running beside the burn on the side of Torr Achilty chasing four or five of the MacDonalds.'

'Ach well,' put in a grey-haired veteran, 'if there were only four or five of them, he should be all right.'

They all laughed at this, though several of them thought that the young lad had maybe bitten off more than he could chew, and they were worried that he might not live to enjoy the glory he had earned that day.

At that there was a noise at the door. They all looked to see what was happening. There stood Big Duncan, one hand holding his axe over his shoulder and the other holding a large bundle. As he stepped forward the light of the fire showed what his bundle was. It was the heads of five MacDonalds strung together on a withy.

'Now tell me that I have not deserved my supper,' he said to Kenneth as he held up the gory prize.

His bold statement was met with gales of laughter and he was provided with as much food and drink as he could eat, which was a lot! From that day onwards he was known as Big Duncan of the Axe.

Now it was said that Duncan was maybe not the full shilling, that he was a little soft in the head, and it is true that Kenneth MacKenzie tended to indulge him as if he were still a child after his great exploits at Blar-na-pairc. About three years later he was with Kenneth at his house at Islandonain. Now Kenneth had received a visitor, an Irishman by the name of Mac a Chruimb, a giant of a man who was notorious for taking advantage of Highland hospitality. He wandered around from chief's house to chief's house partaking of the best food and drink available, well aware that the rules of hospitality ensured he would be well looked after. This wasn't the first time that he had visited Kenneth who had arranged for a small table to be set up for the Irishman with double the amount of food that anyone else was served on his plate. Now Big Duncan was eating with everyone else at the big table and as he ate he was looking over at the visitor. It was well known that Duncan himself was possessed of a great appetite and he was looking longingly at the amount on the Irishman's plate.

At last he could bear it no longer, and standing up he carried his stool over to the Irishman's table and sat beside him. He then drew out his sgian dubh and proceeded to help himself to the double portion.

'What is it you think you are doing?' asked the flustered Irishman, 'that you just come along and help yourself?'

'Well I was thinking,' replied Duncan, with his mouth full, 'that I have an appetite as big as your own.' 'Well,' said the Irishman a bit ominously, 'we shall have to see what we shall see.'

At that the pair of them fell on the food, each seeking to eat as much as possible before the other got it. Soon the platter was clean and Duncan got up and walked off without a word.

Mac a Chruimb though, had something to say. Walking up to Kenneth at the head of the bog table he said, 'Forgive me, but I have travelled amongst all the clans of Scotland and dined in all their chiefs' houses, and I have been well treated here in the past, but I never have been so affronted in all my life as I have been here tonight.'

Now Kenneth was well aware that his visitor had dined in nearly every chief's house in Scotland and that many of them would be happy if they never again found him knocking at their door. However, even if Duncan had been close to abusing the rules of hospitality, he did have a very spot for him.

'Well, as to that, I am sorry, but Duncan is not as other men, and sometimes he does have the habit of playing the fool. He meant no real harm I can assure you,' he said trying to calm the Irishman down.

'Well, that is as may be, came the reply,' but he is certainly no fool at eating, but I will not be made a fool of. I think he and I should have a pass or two at wrestling.'

Now everyone present knew of the giant Irishman's prowess at this sport. In fact it was rumoured that he had killed a couple of men with his bare hands in fights. This however was a direct challenge, and there was no way that Kenneth could stop it going ahead without losing face himself.

So Duncan was sent for and asked if he would wrestle the angry Irishman. 'Och, that I will,' said the young man, 'I was well up with him at eating and see no reason why it won't be the same at wrestling.'

So they fell to. Now the Irishman was a very big man indeed, but Duncan was just about as big and, as it turned out, even stronger. Within a matter of minutes he had thrown the Irishman three times on his back! This only infuriated the visitor further and he demanded that the pair of them should test each other at putting the stone, a pastime still popular at the Highland Games today. Yet again the Irishman was outdone and Duncan beat his best throw by a fair length.

'I have never met my equal before this day in Ireland, England or Scotland,' the Irishman said, with an attempt at being gracious, 'but I think we should go and see who is the better swimmer.' He was still hoping to save the day by proving himself better than Duncan at something.

'Well, why not indeed,' replied Duncan, 'that seems like a good idea to me!' He had no intention of letting the Irishman know that he couldn't swim a stroke.

So the pair of them and a good crowd of the locals went down to the seashore. As soon as they were close Duncan whipped off his plaid and shirt and dived buck naked into the sea which was about twenty feet deep at that point. He disappeared under the water only to bob up to the surface a few seconds later. As soon as he surfaced he called out to a young laddie among the crowd.

'Lachlan will you be doing me favour lad?' he shouted. 'Run off up to the big house an' get a coggie of butter and two or three cheeses for me, all right?' As the young lad nodded and turned to run off to the house Mac Chruimb looked puzzled.

'What are you wanting the butter and cheese for?' he asked Duncan. 'Och, I think we will be needing at least that if we are going to swim over the Kyle,' Duncam responded, treading water. 'I thought we could just swim out to that island over there,' and he pointed to a distant speck of land.

'What?' asked the astonished Irishman, well aware of the treacherous reputation of the currents in the sea between them and the island. 'Do you intend swimming all the way out there? I was meaning to have a few races along the coastline here,' he stuttered.

'Well now,' replied Duncan, 'it was you that gave me the challenge. Wherever I go you must go too,' he said.

The look on the Irishman's face said it all and he made no move to take off his clothes. At this the crowd burst into laughter, most of them well aware that Big Duncan couldn't even swim his own length. Truth to tell he was having a wee bit difficulty just treading water, but there was no way he was going to let the visitor cotton-on to that.

At that Kenneth MacKenzie called on Duncan to come out of the water and let the Irishman off. Duncan came out of the water and standing there naked he was truly a magnificent specimen of a man.

'Well though,' he said, 'if he does not take his own challenge he is perpetually in my debt, is he not?' asked Duncan with a menacing look.

Kenneth, barely able to stop himself laughing, said, 'Well, we'll see about that tomorrow. Just you get dressed and we'll settle things later.' At that he turned and went back to the house, the Irishman following close on his heels, eager to get away from this madman as quickly as he could. All around them people shook with laughter and Duncan looked at them all fiercely, for a moment, then he too let out a giggle.

Come the morning when things were to be settled as to what the Irishman's obligations to Duncan were, there was no sign of him. He had crept away like a thief in the night, and from then on everybody knew that though he was a bit odd, and saw the world differently from other people, there was no way that Big Duncan of the Axe could ever be mistaken for a fool. And as for Kenneth, sure that he would never see the gluttonous Irishman again, his affection for Duncan became even stronger.

The Battle of the Shirts

One of the traditions of clan society that was thought to help strengthen the clan was fostering. Sons of the chief would be sent to other clan families to be raised from childhood through to late adolescence. This meant that they had the equivalent of two families, foster brothers being every bit as loyal as one's own immediate kin were, and even more so, as an old Highland saying shows: 'Kindred to twenty degrees, fosterage to a hundred.' It was an integral part of clan society, and there are many stories of the enduring loyalty and support of foster-brothers to various chiefs. Fostering the son of a chief or someone with more status in clan society was not seen as duty but an honour, and families who fostered chiefs' sons were accorded great respect. In a society where there never was a great deal of physical wealth, such respect was of inestimable value and there were always families keen to foster. However, sometimes the fostering was done outside the clan, and while this was intended to prevent possible feuding it didn't always work.

Now one of the best known instances of fostering going wrong was that of Ronald Gallda [Stranger] MacDonald. He was sent off as a boy to be brought up amongst the Frasers who lived around Glenmoriston. Obviously his father thought that by bringing him up amongst the Frasers the ties between the two clans would be strengthened and he would never have to worry about being raided by the Frasers. Sadly, things did not work out as intended. On receiving the news of his father's death Ronald returned to the MacDonald lands at Castle Tioram. Here a great feast awaited him. The investiture of a new chief was an event of considerable importance, and the whole clan had gathered to put on the best possible show for Ronald. There was what amounted to a small herd of cattle being roasted on spits over fires and there were other fires roasting whole deer from the hill when he arrived, and the people had brought mountains of freshly baked bread and great bowls of butter and cheese. There was a cornucopia of all the best and finest food and a great deal of drink. It was the very best that the clan lands could provide and everyone was in a great state of excitement. They had had the funeral of the old chief with all due solemnity, but now was the time for celebration and the investiture of a new young chief. Opportunities for large-scale celebrations were rare enough and everybody was intent on having a good time. Ronald arrived with a group of his Fraser foster-brothers, having been met at the edge of the Clanranald clan lands by his younger brothers and his uncles. As they came to the field where the feast had been prepared, Ronald looked around him and said: 'You know, you shouldn't have gone to this much trouble and laid on all this food. A few hens would have done just as well.' His remark was met by a deadly silence, and as he looked around with a puzzled expression on his face he began to realise something had gone wrong, very wrong. Whispers were running through the assembled MacDonalds and all levity disappeared as the entire crowd fell silent. Ronald looked at his brothers and uncles. All were staring grim-faced at him and he realised that several of them had drawn their swords.

He could hear someone saying 'We want nothing to do with a hen-chief, this man is not for us.'

Another voice spoke: 'Aye, he has been brought up too close to the Lowlands and has forgotten our ways here.' He looked to his foster-brothers but they were as perplexed as he was.

And then one of his uncles spoke: 'We will be taking you back to the border, Ronald Gallda, you are not fit to be our chief.'

It was a sombre band of men that rode back to the border of Clanranald territory – Ronald's brothers and uncles, accompanied by a further couple of dozen heavily-armed MacDonalds. At the border they told him to go and return no more. He had shamed himself and the entire clan. Maybe it was being brought up by the Frasers, some thought, that had led to this, but what he had done was unforgivable. The investiture of a chief wasn't about the individual, but was for the whole clan. This was an ancient sacred rite that also allowed a much appreciated feast of celebration for every member of the clan. And as the chief he should have been more aware of that than anyone. From that day Ronald Gallda has gone down in tradition as the Hen Chief of the MacDonalds, a fine joke for their enemies and a stain on the honour of his clan. One of his brothers was appointed to be chief in his place. But this was not the end of the affair.

Ronald Gallda's father's plan for peace between Clanranald and the Frasers had achieved the opposite effect. The MacDonalds were so incensed at Ronald's actions that they called on the Camerons to join them in a raid on the Fraser lands. They considered that Lovat, head of the Frasers, had failed in his fostering responsibilities and that all the Frasers should be made to pay for this insult. The Camerons were always ready for raiding and were happy to join them.

A combined force of the MacDonalds and Camerons fell on the Fraser lands around Glenmoriston. Such were their numbers that the Frasers could only retire to the hills and look down as their cattle were rounded up and many of their homes set alight. Lovat, the chief of the Frasers, was already incensed with Clan Ranald for their spurning of his foster son and this incursion only made maters worse. In order to protect himself against possible future reprisals he sent word to the Earl of Huntly, the chief of the Gordons and the king's representative, asking for his support. Huntly was happy to oblige and proceeded west with a large force of MacPhersons and Grants. As they approached Lochaber it seemed likely that there would be a major battle. At this point the Clan Ranald were approached by Campbell of Argyll, who suggested that matters could be settled without a fight if some of the booty was returned. Both he and Huntly were aware that a major battle between Clan Ranald and the Camerons on the one side and the Frasers and their allies from Clan Chattan on the other, could easily escalate. All the other Mac-Donalds and the rest of Clan Chattan, a confederation of several clans, could be drawn in and the whole of the Highlands could erupt into something like a Civil War.

With the promise of most of the lifted cattle being returned, Huntly agreed to withdraw. He offered to accompany Lovat and his Fraser clansmen home, but the offer was refused and the Mackintoshes and Grants headed eastwards. Lovat and his men advanced towards the head of Loch Lochy and homewards. Ronald Gallda had gone on ahead of them. Reaching the clachan of Letterfinlay Lovat was informed that the Clan Ranald were coming over the hills to meet him. There was no way to avoid them, and there at the head of Loch Lochy the two clans met. It was the third of July and a very hot day. Because of the heat Lovat and his men stripped off their plaids and fought, clad only in their shirts. Many of their enemies did the same. Even those who were wearing body-armour threw off their protection in the cloying heat. And as the battle surged more and more of them stripped down to their saffron-coloured shirts. At first there was an exchange of arrows, but once all the shafts had been fired the traditional hand-to hand fighting of the Highlands commenced. Some on both sides had primitive early firearms and once their single shot had been fired they were used like clubs. Others were using the claymore, the great two-handed sword, five feet in length, that had been the favourite weapon of Scottish warriors for so many centuries. Others yet were using the shorter basket-handled swords with the targe, or shield, on their left arms. Neither side would ever give way and the slaughter was dreadful. As weapons were dropped or broken, men fell on each other armed only with their dirk, that ubiquitous Highland weapon and tool, with its foot-long triangular and razor-sharp blade.

Lovat, chief of the Frasers was badly wounded and saw that the battle was going to go on and on with no hope of quarter from his enemies. His own kin, the Frasers were in no mood to be merciful either, and was clear that most of the participants were set on fighting to the death. One of the Frasers was sent after Ronald Gallda to let him know what was happening and to tell him to get away as far as possible from his own kin. When he heard that his foster-father was in trouble he wasted no time in coming back to the battle raging on the shores of Loch Lochy. On reaching the scene of carnage Ronald found Lovat off to one side of the battle, with a large wound in his side and obviously dying.

'Ronald, for heaven's sake,' gasped Lovat, 'begone from here and avenge me later. We have little hope of victory here this day.'

'No father,' said Ronald, as he knelt and took his foster-father's hand. 'You have been a true father to me and I will not desert you on this day.'

So saying, he kissed the dying Lovat and went forward into the thick of the battle. He fought well against his own kin that day, and it is a fact that no one on the Clan Ranald, then or later, ever questioned Ronald's courage, and he killed several of them before coming up against a man called Donald Ruadh Bheg [Wee Red Donald]. Now this Wee Red Donald had a reputation. It had been said of him, unlike most Highland warriors, that he was not as brave as he could be.

Now Donald understood that Ronald Gallda, despite his exhaustion on this hot day, was a far better swordsman than himself and was liable to beat him. And so the red-headed man resorted to as old a trick as exists. As he came at Ronald he shouted, 'Behind you, Ronald!'

Ronald turned, expecting to see another of his clansmen coming at him, but there was no one there. Donald took his chance and stabbed Ronald Gallda right through his chest. It was a death blow, but Ronald in a final burst of fury lashed out backwards and caught his assailant a strong blow on the head. Both of them fell to the heather. After the battle Donald was found to be alive and was carried back to Strontian where he was put to bed, under the charge of a surgeon who had been brought in to help the vast numbers of wounded. He soon regained consciousness and began telling all who came near him how he had seen off the obnoxious hen-chief all by himself. However, his treacherous behaviour had been noticed and there was a great deal of ill-feeling towards him. Ronald Gallda had gone against the clan, but that was no reason be a back-stabber. But Donald would not shut up, clearly looking to be considered some kind of hero.

The upshot of this was that a sum of money – no one knows how much or who gave it – was handed over to the surgeon to ensure that Donald never rose from his sick bed. It was only a day or so after this that the surgeon, wilfully or not, while changing the dressing on his charge's scalp tore the wound open again. Roaring in pain Donald reached for his dirk, and grabbing it he stabbed the surgeon through the heart. The exertion caused his wound to burst even further, and before anyone had time to do anything about it he bled to death. Some say only 4 Frasers out of 300 were left alive and only 10 or so of more than 400 MacDonalds, and there were scores of dead amongst the allies of both clans. The dreadful carnage, with hundreds of bodies strewn in the heather wearing nothing but their saffron shirts was what gave the battle its name *Blar-na-leine* – the Battle or Field of the Shirts. A dreadful price was paid for that off-the-cuff remark of Ronald Gallda, the day he was denied the leadership of his clan.

There were those who saw behind the slaughter the dark hand of the Earl of Huntly himself, who had much to gain by the weakening of two such powerful clans. However these were nothing but suspicions, and nothing was, or could be proved. It is also said that when the Frasers set off for that fateful battle some eighty of them left pregnant wives behind them. Each and every one of them gave birth to sons, which meant that the clan strength could rebuild some of the damage done on the Field of the Shirts.

The Battle of Mulroy

In 1688 the festering troubles between the Mackintoshes and the MacDonells of Keppoch broke out in open war. The MacDonnells at the time held the lands of Glen Spean and Glen Roy which the Mackintoshes thought should be rightfully theirs. In order to help press their claim they took the step of approaching King James IV to ask for a royal charter for these lands. Now like all the Scottish kings James was keen on giving out royal charters for lands that had been held since time immemorial by various clans *a ghlaive* – by the sword. Granting a charter for lands had several advantages for the king. It put the clan chief into his debt and gave him a basis for absorbing another of Scotland's troublesome tribes into the legal system. Once the land had a charter a precedent had been set for the future. The other main advantage was that giving a charter for disputed lands to one of the claimants was guaranteed to set one clan against another, and the kings always reckoned that keeping the fighting amongst themselves might lead to a weakening of the constant danger that the armed forces of the clans always presented to centralised authority. This is a blatantly cynical approach, but why should kings have been any different from modern politicians when it comes to furthering their own power and interests?

The clans themselves rarely bothered to think about long-term political developments, with the notable exception of the Campbells of Argyll, and they were usually concerned with what was important to them at the moment. And land was always important. The more land, the more cattle, the more cattle, the more warriors, the more warriors the more powerful and important the clan would become. And even the humblest of the clansmen was proud of his birth and his kin and considered himself the equal of any other Highland gentleman. So while the clans were rarely led by men obsessed with gaining control over more land, if the opportunity arose to claim more territory then no chief would ignore it. At this time the Keppoch MacDonnells were led by Coll of the Cows, a man whose reputation for raiding and lifting cattle was unsurpassed. That he was a capable strategist and a notable warrior was just part of what such a reputation entailed amongst the clans.

On receiving a demand from the Mackintosh to cede the disputed lands because of the king's charter, duly inscribed on a manuscript made from sheepskin, Coll's reply was terse. The actual words were: 'I hold this land not by a sheepskin but by the sword.' This was the challenge the chief of Mackintosh was waiting for. He had known fine well that the granting of a charter from the king would be seen not just as irrelevant by the MacDonnells, but as a calculated insult. With the help of a considerable number of troops provided by the king he invaded the lands of Glen Roy with a force of around 1,000 men, a considerable number in terms of most clan struggles. They came to Keppoch House only to find it and the surrounding clachans deserted of all men of fighting age. The only people to be seen were women and children, none of whom would say anything concerning the whereabouts of the MacDonnells' fighting forces. However, by the judicious use of a bag of silver Mackintosh managed to find out that the MacDonnells, with a number of their cousins from Glengarry, were encamped in the hollow behind Mulroy.

Night was beginning to fall and Mackintosh decided to climb the mountain in the dark. This, he figured, would put them above the MacDonnels and he would be able to sweep down on them at dawn in the traditional Highland charge. However, he had not considered that the informant who had told him where the enemy were, might have had an ulterior motive. It soon became clear what that motive was. As the Mackintoshes and the government troops came towards the summit just before dawn they could hear that there were already men on the summit. As dawn broke the Keppoch men came down on the Mackintoshes, one eyewitness, a government soldier, alleging later that they came down the hill without either shoe, stocking or bonnet on their heads. The pipe tune composed after the battle says it all in its name: 'MacDonald Took the Brae on Them'. Mackintosh was trapped – if he and his men tried to flee they would be cut down from behind. All they could do was try and withstand the charging warriors screaming down on them. It was a vicious and hard-fought battle. Despite the advantage of the slope the MacDonnells were outnumbered and as the hand-to-hand battle surged victory seemed beyond them. Apart from the sword and targe fighting, there were muskets used and some of the MacDonnells were still using bows and arrows. Back and forth the tide of battle swayed. It finally turned with the arrival of An Baothalan, a simple-minded MacDonnell who was usually to be found tending cattle. His lack of concentration as a child had made him a poor pupil when it came to training in arms, but he had grown into a veritable giant. And, like many of his kind, more then ordinary strength seemed to have compensated for the lack of thinking power.

He had not been summoned to the battle but had turned up anyway, carrying a large wooden club which was little more than a roughly trimmed tree branch. He had never been properly trained in the use of sword and targe because of his condition. He piled into the Mackintoshes and received a musket ball in his shoulder for his trouble. Driven mad with the pain he turned into a killing machine. Like an old-fashioned berserker he ran deep into a group of Mackintoshes with this long wooden club and began mowing them down as if they were no more than a field of standing corn. On seeing this, the rest of the MacDonnells took further heart and surged again. Superior numbers were to no avail as the battle turned inexorably and the Mackintoshes began to flee the field. Their standard-bearer fled – always a sign of defeat – and the place where he jumped across the Roy River to escape his pursuers is still called MacKintosh's Leap. The charter written on sheepskin had not withstood the power of the sword, though the time would come when words on white paper would render the use of the sword an irrelevance. But that time was still a long way off on that day in 1688.

The Loch of the Sword

About three miles north of Rannoch Station at the edge of Rannoch Moor is Lochan a' Claidhcimh [the Wee Loch of the Sword]. To the east lies Beinn Pharlagan, part of the great ridge of Drumalbain, and to the west and north lie the wild and windswept areas of the notorious Rannoch Moor. At first glance this is an inhospitable and dangerous landscape, but it has long been used by the Highland clans to raise cattle, and even as late as the eighteenth century it was a notorious area for cattle-raiders. Here the wildest of the raiders would gather at the end of summer to celebrate the ways of the School of the Moon. It was here that the last Jacobites, carrying on their desperate last stand into the 1750s, would retreat to hide from the Red Army of the British government. Back in the sixteenth century this part of Rannoch was disputed by Locheil, the chief of the Clan Cameron and Atholl, the head of the Robertsons – the Clan Donnachaidh. For many years battles raged over Rannoch and many Highland warriors breathed their last in this wild landscape. Both Locheil and Atholl were tired of the ongoing battle, and it was finally agreed that negotiation rather than battle might be the best way to settle the question of who had control over Rannoch. Through intermediaries – for despite the ongoing feuds between Highland clans there were always family connections to be found – it was arranged that the two of them should meet on a particular day at Lochan a Claideimh. The arrangement was for them each to arrive alone and try to hammer out some kind of settlement.

On the appointed day Cameron set out across the moor. On the way he met a frail-looking old woman on the moor. He wasn't sure that he knew her but she surely knew her clan chief.

'Where are your men, Locheil?' she demanded.

'Ach, I have no need of my men today, mother,' said Cameron. 'A good day to you.' He made to go past her, but she blocked his way.

'Where are your men, Locheil?' the question came again.

'I have no need of men, woman,' he replied, a little irritated by her insistence, 'I am meeting with Atholl alone on the moor. Good day to you,' and so saying he made to move around her and continue his journey towards the meeting place.

The old woman was not done with him though, and as he made to pass her she caught him by his plaid for the third time. In a loud voice she asked him: 'Where are your men, Locheil?'

Pulling himself away from her Locheil carried on, but he

could hear her repeating the question over and over again. He hadn't gone more than a hundred yards or so when the thought came that if anything did go wrong at his meeting with Atholl, he would have been a fool to ignore such an insistent warning. Many old women were reputed to have considerable powers, and this one might be one of those with the second sight. So, turning back toward the old woman still standing where he had left her repeating her mantra, he bowed to her and set off at a brisk pace for the nearest clachan. Here he gathered up every available man, over three dozen of them, and told them to follow him at a distance and to make sure and keep themselves hidden from sight. Tartan plaids in those days were less lurid than they are now and they were in fact extremely good camouflage. The men had all been raised in the arts of raiding, so this was straightforward for them. Their instructions were simple. They were to remain hidden while their chief spoke with the head of the Clan Robertson, but if he exposed the inside of his cloak they were to come at once, sword in hand, to where he stood. Then he advanced to the lochan to meet Atholl.

'A good day to you, Locheil, you are late,' smiled Atholl.

'A good day to you too,' he replied, 'I am sorry for the delay, but I had to stop and listen to one of my clansfolk on the way who had something she wanted to tell me. My apologies, Atholl.'

'Well then, let's to business,' the other replied.

So the negotiations opened, but it soon became clear that Atholl was in no way prepared to give anything away. This just made Cameron all the more determined to stick to his ground. Becoming exasperated with Cameron Atholl lifted off his bonnet and waved it. At that, out of the heather little more than 100 yards away, sprang twenty full-armed Robertsons.

'And who are these?' asked Locheil waspishly.

'Ach well,' sneered Atholl, 'these are Atholl wethers, who have come to graze on Locheil's pastures.'

At that Locheil threw back his cloak and down the slope above the lochan fifty Camerons came running, swords in hand. The original group had been followed by even more men who had been told of what was happening. Taken aback, Atholl blurted, 'And who are these, Locheil?'

'Ach well, these are Locheil's dogs, sharp of tooth and hungry. They are keen indeed to taste the flesh of your Atholl wethers. You would be better now to renounce your title to these lands before matters proceed further, for I doubt if I can control my dogs much longer.'

Realising that he had been out-smarted Atholl had no choice but to agree. Having acceded to Locheil's demands he drew his sword, and swearing on its blade that as long as the sword lay in the lochan this would be Cameron land, he kissed the blade and threw the sword into the lochan. This is probably the most serious oath any Highlander could ever take – swearing on his dirk. The hold of tradition was strong in the Highlands, and still is in some ways, but back in the nineteenth century a young lad fishing in the loch dragged up an ancient basket-hilted sword and handed it over to the local minister. On hearing the news, groups of Camerons came from far and near to insist that the sword be returned, believing that Atholl's promise would be no longer binding. By then though, the lands had been taken over by people who, no matter their name and vaunted pedigree, had no more concern for people than for sheep and deer, but in their hearts the Camerons still held to the old ways.

No Honour Here

A Talented Man

Every age throws up people of remarkable talents who come to prominence. Some become role-models for generations afterwards, but some, by the nature of their character, end up with reputations as out-and-out scoundrels. One of the latter was Simon Fraser, born in 1667. Like many of the sons of the chiefs and lesser chieftains of the clans he was sent off to university at a young age and graduated from Aberdeen in 1687. It is said that he contemplated becoming a lawyer, a profession in which his talents would no doubt have ensured him great success, but it was not to be. This was partially due to the fact that because of his Highland background he was not possessed of the necessary money to spend time as a legal apprentice, and perhaps also that he was not exactly the sort of young man who was much devoted to the idea of hard work!

He decided that he could best make his way in the world through his own clan. The current chief of the Frasers, known as the Lord Lovat, does not seem to have been a strong character and was easily manipulated by the ever-charming Simon, his nephew. By some means or another he managed to get the chief to declare Simon's father as his heir, the chief's only child being a girl. The plan was clearly to give Simon control over the entire clan and the substantial Fraser lands. It is perhaps not surprising that the chief died soon after this, though of course no suspicion can be attached to Simon. He now took the title of Master of

Lovat: after all, his father was the new Lord Lovat. In order for his plan to work he now intended to marry the daughter of the late chief, but as she was only about nine years old at the time this was frowned on by the rest of the clan. At this point certain aspects of Simon Fraser's character become clear. Thwarted by not getting to marry the young lass, he decided that the old adage of there being more than one way to skin a cat should be his watchword! If he couldn't marry the daughter as he had intended, well, her widowed mother would do just as well. After all, Amelia was still just thirty-one years old. The thought that she might feel she should have some say in the matter was not something Simon even contemplated. He was as ruthless as he was charming, and once he was set on a course of action he followed it!

So he got together some of his more amoral accomplices and made a night raid on Doune Castle, the home of the Dowager Lady Lovat. He had taken the precaution of bringing along a minister. This was Robert Munro of Abertarff who had been bundled from his bed and dragged along with Simon and his four companions. He was left in no doubt as to what was being demanded of him, the point being emphasised with a loaded pistol. The Dowager was awakened in the middle of the night when half a dozen armed men burst into her bed-chamber. The two maids who were sleeping there along with her were thrown out and Simon got down to business.

As she awakened the poor woman realised that Simon had every intention of forcing her to marry him there and then. She started to cry and moan, so one of the band of ruffians struck up a tune on the pipes he was carrying for just such an eventuality, and at the point of a sword the Reverend Munro was forced to go through a marriage ceremony between Fraser and the distraught Amelia. She in fact declared that she would rather die than submit to Simon's advances, but she wasn't given the option. Once the words of the service had been read out she was roughly thrown on the bed by Hutcheson Oig and Hugh Fraser of Kilmanovic who proceeded to tear off her dress and slice through the cords of her stays, or corsets. A brutal consummation of the marriage followed – a deed that sent the poor woman half-mad for a time. Having achieved his desired result Simon sent her off to an island in a nearby loch to keep her out of the way for a while. It is one of those strange and almost unbelievable quirks of human nature that eventually the woman actually grew to love the man who had raped her at sword-point in such a travesty of the marriage sacrament.

Simon now reckoned that his position in Clan Fraser was unassailable. He was the son of the current chief and the husband of the late chief's wife, giving him the role of stepfather to the daughter. His plan seemed to be working out well, and he would in time have total control over the clan and all its lands. However, the Reverend Munro and the Dowager's two maids had no intention of letting matters lie, and they reported Simon to the authorities with the immediate effect of having him outlawed. The marriage however was not annulled. His father, no doubt shamed by all this, travelled to Skye, where he soon died, leaving Simon, the outlaw, as Lord Lovat and head of Clan Fraser. These events took place in 1699.

Like many another Highlander before, and like many later, Simon made for the Continent in order to escape the law. At this point the would-be king James VII had set up a court in exile at St Germain, near Paris, and Simon at once headed there to pay his respects to the man he claimed to be his true sovereign. Now the Jacobite court on the Continent was always a hotbed of spying and subterfuge, and by declaring his undying support for the Stewart cause Simon was promised full restitution of all the Fraser lands in the event of James VII regaining his throne. His charm had worked again. His next action, however, shows us his true character.

The current king of England and Scotland, William III, the

one-time Duke of Orange, was visiting some of his own lands in the Low Countries at the time and hot-footing it from St Germain Simon went to visit him. Not a man to hang about when an opportunity presented itself, Fraser gained admittance to see the king and using his famous charm, he convinced William that he had been 'fitted-up' and the king granted him a pardon. Now it is always difficult to be sure what double-dealing desperadoes are up to, but there is little doubt that when it came to duplicity Simon was in a class of his own. He kept a foot in both camps and in 1703 he was asked by James VII to find out how many of the Highland chiefs were likely to come out on the Stewart side in any future struggle. As a clan chief in his own right he seemed to be just the man for this job, but finding there was not at this time a great willingness amongst the Highlanders to support the Stewarts, he promptly told what he knew to the British Governent of Queen Mary, William having recently died.

However, he was nothing if not brazen, and a while later he returned to the Jacobite court. The world of Scottish politics in particular was a small one and word of Simon's even-handed-ness towards both sides got out. The result was that he was locked up in the castle of Angouleme in 1703 by the Jacobites. He was to spend almost the next ten years of his life in the castle, something you might think would teach him a lesson or two. Or maybe not. True at least to his own idea of himself, he managed to escape and return to Scotland in 1714. It says a lot about his powers of persuasion that he was involved, at least briefly, with the Jacobites in the abortive rising of 1715, but he managed to stay well clear of any prisons this time, possibly by supplying intelligence to the Hanoverian Government, the house of Saxe-Coburg now having been handed the thrones of Britain by the recently created government of the United Kingdom.

For a while after this Simon seemed to be concerning himself with more domestic matters, though it wasn't that long before his character showed again. He concluded that he had had enough of his current wife and decided that the time had come for a new one! He was now approaching fifty years of age. Somehow, after arranging for the marriage to be annulled – which must have cost a bit in those days – he convinced Margaret, the daughter of the Laird of Grant, to take him on. She soon bore the old rascal a son, and it is a measure of the man's sheer chutzpah that the godfather of his son and heir was none other than George I. No one could ever accuse Simon Lovat of a lack of style.

He was not finished with marriage however, as he still had an eye for the ladies. Margaret died and, at the age of 66, he decided he needed a new wife. His eye fell on the daughter of Campbell of Mamore, Primrose, a beautiful young woman who had far too much sense to listen to the blandishments of an old rogue like Simon. But, as had been evident so often before, once Simon was set on something it was hard to put him off. It wasn't long after she had sent him packing that the young lady got a note telling her that her mother, who was staying in Edinburgh at the time, was close to death. The fact that it was a strange address gave her no concern; she was simply distraught to learn of her mother's illness and made her way as quickly as she could to the address in Edinburgh's High Street. Once she was admitted to the house she realised that something was amiss. There, awaiting her in the hall, was none other than Simon Lovat, and all around him were gaudily dressed and heavily painted females. It looked like a brothel. Her mother was, of course, fit and well in a nearby house, unaware that her daughter was even in Edinburgh. Simon wasted no time in telling her that it was truly a brothel and that by entering its doors she had played right into her hands. If she did not consent to marry him there and then he would destroy her reputation within hours and no man would ever come near her again! The old dog was up to his tricks again. This blatant blackmail had the desired effect on the poor young woman, and she entered into marriage with the despicable old roué. Not long after this she bore him a son, after which she had the good sense to flee from the clutches of her persecutor!

Now while Simon was up to his old tricks the country continued to be racked by plot and counter plot as the exiled Stewarts worked to regain their thrones. Things came to a head in 1745, when Prince Charles Edward Stewart landed at Glenfinnan on the West Coast and a few clans came to support him. Not long after that the Jacobites won a stunning victory over the government troops at Prestonpans, a victory still celebrated in the song 'Hi Johnnie Cope'. This seemed to be the sign that Simon was waiting for, and he wholeheartedly threw his support behind the Young Pretender. After a lifetime of intrigue and subterfuge he was now clearly on the Jacobite side. Or was he? His own advanced age and ill-health made him useless as a soldier, but he sent his son with a contingent of Fraser clansmen to join the Prince. As ever, he tried to play both sides. He then sent word to Lord President Forbes, the government's chief supporter in Scotland, that his son had taken the troops out despite him, and that he was as loyal as ever to the house of Hanover. Forbes was not fooled.

After the dreadful slaughter at Culloden he realised that retreat to the mountains was inevitable. After watching his own castle at Dounie being brought down he contacted the other Jacobite leaders to urge that a guerrilla-type force of 3,000 men should be gathered together in the Highlands to carry on the fight. Using their knowledge of the terrain they could cause enough trouble to the government to be able to sue for decent terms of peace. This did not happen though there were scattered bands who fought on for almost a decade. As for Simon, he was carried off in a litter to the west where before long he was captured on an island in Loch Morar. And some stories say that he had a sum of 6,000 guineas with him! This was no doubt some of the money destined to support the Jacobite struggle that somehow ended up in his possession. His long, if varied, service as a government informer was to do him no good. After a short period of imprisonment at

Fort Augustus the old campaigner was taken by coach to London, in easy stages due to his advanced age. The authorities wanted to make sure that he came to trial. Given the virtual ethnic cleansing being carried on in the Jacobite parts of the Highlands by the Red Army of the British Government, the verdict, and his sentence, were inevitable.

Gulity, and death by beheading, as befitted a man of his standing in society! Lesser rebels were condemned to be hung, but Simon as ever had to do things in style. And this he certainly did. On the way to the execution dock at Tower Hill, a Cockney woman leapt onto the running board of the carriage, and sticking her head through the window shouted: 'You're going to get your head chopped off, you ugly old Scotch dog.' Simon smiled sedately at her and retorted, 'I verily believe I shall, you ugly old English bitch.'

A few minutes later, as he ascended the scaffold before the gathered crowds he was the very picture of calm. Being helped towards the scaffold steps by a couple of his jailers, he looked around and commented, 'God save us, why should there be such a bustle about taking off an old grey head that can't get up three steps without two men to support it?'

Once on the scaffold he approached the executioner and tested the sharpness of the axe with his thumb. To the appreciative cheers of the crowd he then tipped the axeman a guinea and, quoting a Latin tag from Horace – *Dulce et decorum est pro patria mori* (It is sweet and honourable to die for one's country) – he calmly knelt down and laid his head across the block. The axe fell and the long and incredible life of Simon, Lord Lovat, was at last over. Typically of him, it turned out that he was the very last person to be beheaded in Britain. A showman to the last.

The False Bride

There is a fine old Scots Ballad called 'The Fause [or False] Bride' in which a young man is slighted in love by his intended.

In that story the young man dies of a broken heart, but there are stories of marriages that are much, much worse than that. Now the Campbells have long had a bad reputation as the most devious and ambitious of all the Scottish clans. The careful politicking of a series of the Dukes of Argyll and their kinsmen eventually led to them being the most powerful of all the clans, though the clansfolk of the Campbells fared no better than those in other areas when the value of livestock began to be held in higher esteem by the lairds than the lives and traditions of their own kin. Much of the reputation has been said by the Campbells to be little more than sour grapes and envy on the part of other clans who did not do so well. The blame laid at their door for the Glencoe Massacre is a case in point. The few Campbells, less than ten per cent of the troops involved, were in fact carrying out the express wishes of the government of the day when they slaughtered the men, women and children of the Glencoe MacDonalds in the deep snows of midwinter in 1692. It was an act of butchery carried out by soldiers of the British army as a deliberate act of government policy and as a warning to other clans.

However, the Campbell name for 'sleekitness' is supported by some of the stories told of them.

In the wars of Montrose, when the Jacobites first rose in Scotland after the installation of William and Mary on the British throne in 1688, one of the Royalists was MacNaughton of Dundarave whose ancestral lands lay on the shores of Loch Fyne, some three miles east of Inveraray in Argyll. On one side his neighbour was Campbell of Inveraray to the west, and to the east Campbell of Ardkinglas; both had long coveted MacNaughton's lands. The estates were forfeited after the first Jacobite rebellion but MacNaughton was soon pardoned and given his lands back. Perhaps the Campbells had missed their chance? Now John MacNaughton had fallen in love with Margaret, the youngest and prettiest of the three daughters of Sir James

Campbell of Ardkinglas. They had met on a few social occasions and John knew, despite the long ongoing feuds between his people and the Campbells, that this was the lass he wanted for his wife. And Margaret had made it clear that she was in total agreement. Perhaps, like many a chief before him, he thought by marrying into his enemy's clan peace could be guaranteed, but that was a bonus, for he truly loved Margaret. But things did not work out quite as the young couple hoped.

First he had to get the permission of her father and it was with a deal of worry that he set out one day for Ardkinglas. He was shown in to the great hall on arrival and there was Sir James himself. Surrounded by his traditional enemies it says a lot for MacNaughton that he boldly entered the castle and with no hesitation came straight to the point.

'Sir James, I love your daughter Margaret and I am sure that she loves me. Despite the problems that have existed for generations between our families I would like your permission to marry her.'

The hall was deadly silent as the clansmen who had accompanied MacNaughton into the hall of the chief fingered the handles of their swords. Was this an insult, or was it an opportunity?

Sitting there with a glass of claret in his hand, Sir James smiled at MacNaughton and said, 'Of course you can have my permission. I have been aware of her feelings for a while, and if she wishes to marry the Chief of the MacNaughtons then she can do so with my blessing.'

John was astounded, but delighted with the reply. He had expected to have to argue for a long while, and this immediate acceptance was much more than he had dared to hope for. Whisky was called for to bless the union and toasts were drunk to the future bride and groom. It was late that night before John MacNaughton collapsed into a bed within the walls of Ardkinglas Castle, a place he had never hoped to spend a night in before!

Preparations were soon under way. This was a major occasion, the daughter of a chief marrying another chief, and everything would have to be just right on the great day. Vast amounts
of the best food money could obtain were shipped in and
fearsome quantities of drink – whisky, wine and ale. On the
appointed day John arrived dressed in his finest clothes and
accompanied by a select band of the finest-looking Highlanders
amongst the MacNaughtons. They were all shown into the main
hall of the Castle where at once a greybeard of whisky was
produced. Drinks were passed around and toasts made and the
MacNaughtons emptied their glasses, which were immediately
refilled. It was a wedding after all. There was to be a meal before
the happy couple were to be married and the groom's party sat
down to a magnificent feast, every dish being accompanied by
copious amounts of whisky or wine. By the time of the ceremony
there was not a MacNaughton, including their chief, who was
not in high spirits and ready for the coming celebrations. In came
the bride wearing a long white veil and the wedding vows were
exchanged. This was immediately followed by a ceilidh which
the MacNaughtons there thought was a true sign that peace
between them and their ambitious neighbours was now settled.
A great time was had by all.

John, who was pretty drunk by this time, was convoyed with
this new bride to a room high up in one of the towers of
Ardkinglas Castle, there to consummate the vows they had just
taken. In the morning he awoke, his head full of vague memories
of the night before. He was sure his beautiful new bride would
forgive him; Highland women knew what their men could be like
in celebration. He laid his hand on her shoulder and turned her
towards him. There, sleeping gently as a baby was Jane, Margaret's older and uglier sister! He had been duped. Campbell
had planned the whole thing months before and had had
Margaret locked up in another room on the morning of the
wedding. Jane had been well rehearsed in what she was to do and

she was only too happy to have the chance of marrying the handsome young chief of the MacNaughtons.

Realising that most if not all of his own people would have gone home the night before, John understood his predicament. Alone in Ardkinglas, surrounded by Campbells and married to the wrong daughter, he resolved to act quickly. He knew that Margaret would not have given in to this evil plot and was sure she must be somewhere in the castle. But she would have come to him to warn him if she could, so she must be locked up somewhere.

Silently flitting through the old castle he at last found a locked door, which he forced with his sgian dubh. As he swung the door open the eyes of his intended bride looked straight at him. There, bound to a chair and gagged was Margaret. He untied her and the two of them clasped each other tightly. Then before the rest of the household was astir they quietly sneaked out.

John had relatives in Ireland that he knew would help. He also realised that if he stayed here he would be forced to live with Jane. That way he might be able to hang onto his ancestral lands, but for how long? His father-in-law had shown just how ruthless he was prepared to be. His choice was simple – his inheritance or the woman he loved. And so John and Margaret turned their back on Scotland forever. Behind them they left an aggrieved new bride and a happy father-in-law. He had reckoned that this ploy would get rid of the young chief, either by forcing him into some hot-headed reaction that could be turned against him or, as had happened, by getting him to flee the country.

The deserted Jane who had been convinced she would be MacNaughton's wife soon found that she was with child, even after one night. In time a fine healthy son was born to her. His grandfather seemed to dote on the boy and once he was walking he often took him fishing. So it was that a few years later he came to the castle with the terrible news that the wee lad had drowned in the Kinglas Water while out fishing! Few had trouble believing that Campbell had a hand in the death of his own grandson. And it was not long after that he applied to have the lands of the MacNaughtons escheated – taken away from his son-in-law – on the grounds that John was an absconding adulterer who was guilty of incest. All of these were serious charges and there was indisputable proof of them all. Once the estates were forfeited to the Crown he claimed them on behalf of his daughter, the legal wife of John, chief of the MacNaughtons – and in this he was successful. Jane was then married to a laird's son who was happy to change his name to Campbell, and so the MacNaughtons lost Dundarave forever and the Campbells' power grew a little more.

The Word of a Campbell

In the aftermath of the battle of Glen Fruin, when the MacGregors were being hunted all across Scotland, Alisdair MacGregor of Glenstrae, who had led the clan in the fateful battle, was in a difficult position. Like the rest of the Highland clansmen he was used to hardship and the tactics of guerrilla warfare that had been in use in Scotland since Roman times stood him in good stead. He and his men were well capable of living off the land and striking hard and fast against their enemies. It was, however, different for the women and children of the clan. The utter persecution of the clan meant that Alisdair's people, like all other MacGregors, were liable to be attacked at any time. The men could live rough, but it was hard on the women and children, and over the following winter many of them fell into a truly pitiable condition. Now Alisdair, like all clan chieftains, was a man of considerable pride. The idea of surrendering to his enemies was one which he found hard to contemplate. He was also aware that his life, like that of many of his immediate relatives, would be forfeit if he surrendered directly to the king. However, the hardship being suffered by the MacGregors tore at his heart and he resolved to do something about it. He believed that if he were to go into exile there was at least a chance that the ongoing persecution of his people would come to an end.

He seems to have been unaware that MacCailean Mor, the head of the Campbell clan, was active in encouraging the persecution of his people and that he had a long-term plan to take over the MacGregor lands. All Highlanders to this day, and even many of those whose ancestors have lived in Scotland's cities for the past few centuries, have an almost mystical love of the Highlands of Scotland. Set against uncertain and often dangerous weather and the hardships of life on what is marginal land, are the stunning beauty of the bens and glens and the ancestry stretching back through generations beyond counting who lived in the same places. Despite these ties Alisdair knew that something had to give. The government was set on destroying his people and there were too many clans ready to help them, whether out of ancient enmity, or, like the Campbells, out of hope for gain – gain of land. As the leader of his own kin Alisdair decided that he would have to come to some sort of terms with the Campbells. He understood that the encouragement that MacCailean Mor had given him to attack the Colquhouns in the period before the Glen Fruin raid had been part of a larger plan, but between one Highland chief and another surely something could be worked out.

The intermediary that he chose was Campbell of Ardkinglas, who held the lands round the head of Loch Fyne. MacGregor's hope was that he and his immediate kin would be allowed to go into exile in England, or even further abroad. As the man who had been blamed by the government for the Battle of Glen Fruin and the attendant slaughter, particulary that of the innocent scholars, he knew well that he could not hope to live long in Scotland. And he thought that since he had had the tacit support of the Campbells in his actions, some kind of arrangement should be possible. In order to discuss the possibilities he accepted an offer to visit Campbell at Ardkinglas.

Arriving with just a couple of men, he was shown into the main room of the castle. Campbell was polite and offered them dinner, and but it was soon clear that the building was full of armed Campbells and that Ardkinglas had no intention of letting Alisdair go.

'In your situation, Alisdair, I think it better that you surrender yourself to me, here and now,' said his host.

'Well then, Ardkinglas,' the MacGregor replied, 'it seems that I have little choice, but I will ask you for your word that you will take me over the English border and let me and my men go free. My family can join me later. I accept I have to leave my lands forever.'

'I promise I will take you to England,' came the reply, 'and here's my hand on it.' And then the two men shook hands to seal the arrangement. This was a terrible price he was paying, but Alisdair had little choice, and when Campbell seemed to accept the deal the pair of them sat down and ate supper together.

The very next day Alisdair and his few followers left Ardkinglas on horseback in the company of a large body of Campbells, all fully armed. Over the next few days they made their way through southern Scotland towards Berwick, where Alisdair was to be set free. You can imagine the disturbance that this large body of armed and mounted Highland clansmen caused as they trevelled across the Lothians and down through the Merse to Berwick. The company then rode through the old border town and into England, where they stopped.

'Well then,' said Alisadair, 'we now part company.'

'I think not,' came the reply, 'I gave you my word that I would bring you to England but now there are some gentlemen awaiting you in Edinburgh.'

Surrounded by armed men, and with no weapons of his own, Alisdair could do nothing. Truth to tell, the Campbell had been very careful in his choice of words. Yet again Alisdair had been outmanoeuvred. At once the company turned around and set out northwards for Edinburgh at a fast pace.

They arrived on 19th January, and the following day, after a night in the dungeons, Alisdair was put on trial with over thirty of his kin. The sentence was a forgone conclusion, and all who were present there knew it. The court, even though they knew the MacGregors were being persecuted on all sides, had no intention of allowing even the distinct possibility of a rescue attempt. They were certain if they did not act at once such an attempt was certain to be organised. So the very next day Alisdair MacGregor of Glenstrae was hung in Edinburgh, together with a number of his own close relatives. In an ironic nod towards his status Alisdair 'wes hung on ane pyn about ane eln heichar nor the rest' – he was hung on a pine an ell – approximately a metre – higher than the rest.

Before he died Alisdair called for paper, pen and ink. In his dying statement he made it clear that his attack on the Colquhouns had been encouraged by MacCailean Mor, the head of the Campbell clan himself. The contents of his statement soon circulated amongst the remaining MacGregors and the fiery cross was sent round the lands that they still held. The entire fighting strength of the MacGregors, disgusted at the treachery and legal murder of Glenstrae, set out for retribution.

They laid the blame squarely at the feet of Duncan Campbell of Glenorchy, who they believed had encouraged MacCailean Mor. They fell on the lands of Culdares and Duneaves in Breadalbane, Glenfalloch and Bochstel in Menteith, and burnt down Duncan's castle at Achallader. It was later calculated that his financial losses were in the region of £70,000, a fortune at the time. After the raid the MacGregors split up and went to ground, never again rising in such force, and many of them found shelter with other clans who sympathised with their plight.

And despite the efforts of the king and of the head of the Campbells the MacGregors survived.

Donald Gorm

The ancient laws of hospitality in the Highlands and Islands were of great cultural significance. It was the custom that any stranger passing should not only be given food, shelter and a bed, but would be under the protection of the host during his stay. Strangers passing through an area could ask hospitality of any house and the clans were always proud of the hospitality visitors would receive if they were put up by the chief. This was part of the ostentation for which Highland chiefs were notorious; they liked to show that they were capable of giving a grand welcome to any and all visitors. Instances where the rules of hospitality were broken were always seen as shocking, but this did not prevent the more unscrupulous from trying to take advantage of the ancient tradition.

Early in the seventeenth century MacLeod of Rodil, Rory Mor, was sporadically fighting with the Clan Ranald, the Mac-Donalds. Specifically, Rory Mor was having an ongoing problem with Donald Gorm MacDonald from Uist. On one occasion Donald Gorm was heading for Uist in his birlinn when the weather in the Minch, never very predictable at the best of times, took a turn for the worse. Like all the clansmen of the Western Isles Donald was a fine sailor and he knew enough not to risk the Minch when it was wild. So he decided to run for shelter to the nearest anchorage, which happened to be Loch Dunvegan, with the castle of his enemy looming over it. It was not the choice he would like to have made.

Maybe Rory Mor didn't realise who his unexpected guest was, at first, for he sent a man out in a wee boat to give his greetings to the crew and invite them to partake of the hospitality of Dunvegan Castle. There was some discussion amongst Donald

Gorm and his crew as to the advisability of accepting this offer – true, it was the custom, but just as true was the fact that the two clans were at feud with one another. However, tradition won over caution – Rory Mor had offered hospitality and Donald Gorm thought it would be beneath him to refuse such an offer. So the MacDonald men made their way to Dunvegan Castle that evening. Truth to tell, Rory Mor had a reputation for treating his guests so well that the nickname of Dunvegan at the time was 'the Fort of the Hospitality of the Wine Cups'. A fine evening's eating and drinking surely lay before them as they approached the Castle. As they entered through the great gate Rory Mor and a group of his own clansmen were already waiting to greet them.

'Good evening, Donald Gorm,' began Rory Mor, 'I welcome you and your men to partake of the hospitality of Dunvegan. Rory Mor, would you like to come and dine with me in my own apartment?'

Tradition or not, Donald Gorm was going to play safe with Rory Mor.

'It is the custom of Donald Gorm when from home,' he said, none too graciously, 'to sit with his own men.'

'Och, they will be well looked after in the main hall,' replied MacLeod, 'but you should come and sit with me at my table.'

'I have said,' repeated Donald, 'that when away from home Donald Gorm always eats in the company of his own men.'

MacLeod tried further to convince his guest that he was showing him honour, but Donald would have none of it. His suspicions of Rory Mor just made him more and more adamant. At last, seeing he would not get his own way, Rory Mor allowed the entire crew, a dozen men, to come and eat in his own apartment. As Rory Mor would hardly seat himself amongst a crowd of MacDonalds alone he also brought in a group of his own clansmen, making it a pretty crowded space! Drink was passed around continuously, the food was of the finest, and the night began to develop into a bit of an occasion. And, as has been said often enough, when the drink flows the tongue loosens. Rory Mor, as fou as anyone else there that night, at one point leaned over the table to address Donald and asked a somewhat pointed question:

'Now, Donald Gorm, let's be having the truth now, did you or did you not kill my father?' the chief asked.

'Well, it has been said of me that I killed three despicable Highlanders,' Donald snapped back, 'and I have no fears of adding a fourth this night if necessary.' Then hauling out his dirk he held it up in his right hand and said, 'This is the dirk that laid your father low. It has a grand point, a firm haft, and its edge is sharper than the serpent's tooth. And I will tell you this it is held by the second-best hand in Skye!'

At this, Rory Mor thought that Donald was seeking to defuse the situation by giving his host a compliment. He was aware that all his own clansmen were sitting tensely and most of them had their right hands on their own dirks. 'So what's the best hand?' inquired his host.

Donald lightly tossed the weapon from his right to his left hand and said ominously, 'This is it.'

There were sharp intakes of breath all round the room, and the MacLeods looked at their chief, who had just been so blatantly insulted. At his word they would have happily fallen on their guests, despite the laws of hospitality. There was no doubt that Donald was pushing things by insulting his host. Rory Mor, however, kept calm, and remembering the rules of hospitality he called for more drink. His clansmen looked at each other, wondering just what their chief had in mind. It was not like him to take an insult of any kind, never mind one given him over his own table! The atmosphere, to put it mildly, was strained.

Soon afterwards it was decided that it was time to go to sleep, and Rory Mor, ever the generous host, offered Donald Gorm a fine bed with lined sheets in one of the private apartments in the castle.

'When from home,' came the phrase, 'Donald Gorm never sleeps apart from his own men.' In truth the idea of a fine comfortable bed was very appealing, but he thought it much safer to stick with his men, especially as he was fully aware of just how much he had offended his host.

It had been decided that the men would sleep in the thatched roofed wooden kiln where corn was laid out to dry after the harvest. It was close to the castle and was snug, with plenty of room for the dozen or so MacDonalds. So the group of them, many considerably drunk, wrapped themselves up in their plaids and lay down to sleep in the kiln. Donald though, despite having downed a fair amount of whisky, had no intention of sleeping a wink. He simply did not trust Rory Mor. It was just before first light when he heard somebody approaching the kiln. He stood just inside the door, dirk in hand, and looked through a gap between the door and the frame as a figure loomed out of the dark.

'Donald, Donald Gorm, are you awake?' came a soft voice. It was an old friend, Duncan MacAskill.

'Aye Duncan, how are you, old friend?' came the reply.

'Och, I am fine but it is yourself that will not be unless you get yourself and your men back on your birlinn, quickly,' whispered Mac. 'There is no time to waste; move now,' and with that he disappeared into the night.

Donald Gorm moved quickly among his men, waking them and signalling that they should move out. This they did, quietly shutting the door behind them, so that it would appear that they were still in the kiln. So it was that just as the first streaks of pre-dawn light crossed the sky, Donald Gorm and his companions made their way down to the shore and swam quietly out to their birlinn. The storm of the previous night had blown itself out and there was an off-shore wind sufficient to allow them to raise sail at once. And as they sailed out of Dunvegan Loch Donald looked back just in time to see a flicker of flame at the door of the kiln. Within seconds the entire building was a mass of flames. As they sailed back round to Sleat Donald was quietly laughing to himself: Rory Mor thought he had got his revenge on Donald Gorm, but his actions had ended up costing him his kiln. And he had also been obliged to lay on a good night's food and drink for the MacDonalds.

Now this escape did nothing to harm Donald's reputation as a clever warrior and a fine leader of men. He was also, like most of the Highlanders, a man in whom bravery could easily turn to foolishness. No true Highlander could bear the thought of being considered less than a fearless warrior. And given the traditional practice of inter-clan raiding there were always plenty of opportunities for them to show just how brave they were. Donald's reputation for bravery was clearly strengthened when word went round of how he had behaved while at Dunvegan. There were some, however, who thought that such bravery bordered on the foolish, and that Donald Gorm had a tendency towards bravado. They had a point.

In 1539, some years after the incident at Dunvegan, Donald Gorm was involved in a feud with MacRae of Inverinate. The MacDonalds had forced MacRae to take refuge in Eilean Donan Castle at the entrance to Loch Duich and decided to attack the ancient stronghold. In those days bows and arrows were still important weapons and both attackers and defenders were using them. MacRae was a more than capable archer himself, and noticing Donald Gorm at the forefront of his men as they attacked he took aim and fired. The arrow pierced Donald Gorm just above the right knee and he fell to the ground. Immediately a couple of his clansmen lifted him up and carried him to his birlinn which they launched from the shore and rowed well beyond the reach of any more arrows. Donald was in considerable pain but considered it beneath his dignity to show any reaction to it.

'Ach, it's nothing,' he said, sitting upright in the boat, 'I'll just have it out now.' He grasped the flight end of the arrow, and before either of his companions could stop him he yanked the weapon from his leg. At once blood began to spout from the wound, and it was clear he had ruptured an artery. At once his men tried to apply a tourniquet, using a sword belt, but with the boat heaving up and down in the waters of the sea-loch as they worked, it took them a few minutes to pull it tight. By this time Donald had lost a great deal of blood and had passed out. The rest of the MacDonalds realised their chief was badly injured and had returned to their birlinns, carrying the bodies of their dead and injured. At once their small armada headed back to Skye. The wind rose against them, and by the time they reached Loch Alsh the waves were a fair height and the boats were being tossed about. Try as they might, Donald Gorm's companions couldn't keep the wound from spurting more and more blood. Soon it was obvious that in these conditions they would never reach the Isle of Uist while Donald still breathed. In their desperation they beached the chief's birlinn on a tidal island in the middle of Loch Alsh. They carried the chief to the bank and there Donald Gorm breathed his last. His bravery had led him to scorn his wound and bring on his own death. So the MacDonalds lost their chief, and ever since then the sandbank has had the name Larach Tigh Mhic-Dhomhnuill, which can be translated loosely as 'the site of MacDonald's House'. And so passed one of the greatest of all the MacDonald warriors.

The Ladies

━━▷◆◁━━

Colonel Anne

Now it is an odd fact that few women take centre-stage in the stories of the clans that survive. They are usually present either as the wives of central characters or occasionally as wise women who are either healers or have some visions of the future. These latter are probably some kind of folk memory of ancient pagan priestesses which no doubt accounts for them sometimes being presented as witches, whether of the black or white variety. There is one particular female however who stands out in the period of the '45. This is Anne Mackintosh, daughter of Farquharson of Invercauld. She married the Mackintosh and lived with him at Moy Hall, ten miles south-east of Inverness. She was not long married and still only twenty years of age when Prince Charlie arrived in Scotland. Now many of the clans were, like the rest of British and Scottish society, split over which side to support – the Hanoverians or the Jacobites. Anne's father was on the Hanoverian side, but she herself was staunchly Jacobite, even though her husband was an officer in the British Army. She called out the clan for Charlie, and there is a description of her at the head of her clansmen 'with a man's bonnet on her head, a tartan riding habit richly laced and a pair of pistols at her saddle bow'. Now she might have ridden out from Moy Hall at the head of the clan, but she was too sensible a woman to take on the command of the clan. This was the responsibility of the clan Captain, Alexander MacGillivary. It had long been a part of clan tradition that the best military leader of the clan should lead in battle, rather than the chief.

At the battle of Prestonpans, where General Cope was so soundly beaten, the Laird of Mackintosh was taken prisoner with his brother-in-law young Invercauld. They were in fact captured by a troop of scouts from Mackintosh's own clan and were taken to Prince Charlie himself. Here Mackintosh gave his word that he would refrain from fighting for a year and was allowed to return home to Moy Hall. On reaching home Aeneas was met at the door by his wife, who curtsied and said 'Your servant, Captain.'

No doubt in honour of her role in bringing out his own clansmen on the side they had long supported, Aeneas bowed low and replied 'Your servant, Colonel.'

Little more is known of Aeneas till after Culloden, but Colonel Anne's main claim to fame arises from the engagement that took place not far from their home at Moy Hall.

It was in February 1746 that Prince Charlie, on his long retreat from England came to Moy Hall, sixteen miles to the south-east of Inverness. He arrived with a small detachment of troops to be welcomed by Anne with all the warmth of traditional Highland hospitality. He had left a larger group of Highlanders under the command of Locheil a few miles to the south. These numbered little more than 500 men.

Now up in Inverness Lord Loudon was in command of a Hanoverian force numbering over 1,500 men, quite a few of them having been brought in by MacLeod of Dunvegan. Amongst them were several who would far rather have been on the Prince's side, and one of them was MacCrimmon, the hereditary piper to Macleod of Dunvegan. Word came to Inverness from Grant of Delachny that the Prince was at Moy Hall and that if a strong force was sent out they would have little trouble in capturing him. This was a very attractive proposition for Loudon, as apart from the kudos it would bring it would effectively put an end to the rebellion if they could capture the chief rebel himself!

So the combined force of government troops and MacLeods set out for Moy from Inverness leaving a strong guard on the gates of Inverness to prevent any word being sent ahead. However, the plans had been overheard by a Mackintosh lass who was serving in the house where Loudon had billeted himself and his general command. Once the troops had left he ran to the nearby home of the Dowager Lady Mackintosh, Anne's mother-in-law and told her what was happening. Like her daughter-in-law, Lady Mackintosh was a Jacobite and realised that something had to be done. She called a young lad of the clan who worked for her, called Lachlan, and told him he had to get out of the town and take word to Moy Hall that the troops were on their way. Now Lachlan Mackintosh was a lad in his early teens who knew his way around Inverness and the hills between the city and Moy Hall as well as anyone. It was an easy task for him to sneak out of the town despite the guards and to head off into the hills.

Lord Loudon's regiment and the contingent of MacLeods were marching south, down the main road, and Lachlan knew how dangerous it would be to try and pass them in the dark. They were liable to have scouts out ahead and behind the main body of troops, and the stars and the crescent moon were giving some light. Still, he would have to cover some of the way on the road – going over the hills in darkness would take just too long. So he headed down the road, keeping his eyes and ears open. He hadn't been going long and had just turned a bend onto a long exposed straight stretch of the highway, when he heard a noise behind him. It sounded like a detachment of horses following the government troops. They were travelling at a fair pace, considering that the only light was that of the moon and stars. The young lad had barely enough time to throw himself into the roadside ditch before the horses came round the bend. Once they were past he dragged himself out of the muddy water and ran as fast as he could after them. He was sure he would hear when they caught up with the main detachment.

It was only a few minutes later when he heard the horses slowing down and a command coming faintly on the night air: 'Halt in the King's name. Who goes there?'

The horsemen had caught up with the troops and Lachlan at once turned to his left and made for the hills. Keeping a couple of hundred yards off the road he moved as quickly as he could Soon he could see the troops with the faint light glinting on the shouldered muskets of Lord Loudon's Regiment. His way was hard, but he was young and fit, and he soon realised that though the soldiers had advance and rear guards set they didn't seem to have any roving patrols parallel to their main body. They were pinning their hopes on getting to Moy Hall quickly and surprising the Jacobites. But speedily as they marched they were no match for a young Highland laddie raised in these hills. Still he had to be careful and it took him some time to catch up and pass the detachment of soldiers and clansmen. At last, he succeeded in passing them and could take to the road. Once back on the road he ran like a hare all the way to Moy Hall, stopping only to drink from roadside burns along the way. As he ran, heavy rain began to fall, and in the distance he could hear the rumble of thunder.

By the time he arrived at Moy, ten long miles from the Highland capital, he was exhausted. The Jacobite troops had no outliers and the first guard he met was only a couple of hundred yards from the Hall overlooking Loch Moy. The first he knew of the guard was when a rough hand grabbed him from behind and he felt a dirk at his throat.

'Who are you, and where are you going laddie?' a voice asked in Gaelic. Replying in the same tongue he said, 'I am Lachlan Mackintosh. There are over a thousand troops coming down the road behind me. They know the Prince is at the Hall. I must tell Lady Anne.'

'Right, come along then,' said the Highlander, releasing him and running alongside him as they approached the sentry stationed at the door of the hall. Within minutes all were awake and Lady Anne was questioning the bedraggled and exhausted young lad.

'How far are they behind, Lachlan?' she asked gently. Outside the hall the prince and his men were already mounting their horses. They were going back to join Lochiel's men and it seemed as if they would have to make a stand a few miles down the road. Anne Mackintosh, however, had a different plan.

'Well, I think they will be more than half an hour yet,' the lad gasped, still trying to recover his breath. 'I ran most of the last few miles.'

'Well done, Lachlan Mackintosh,' Anne said, pressing him gently on the shoulder, 'this will not be forgotten.'

At that she went outside to say farewell to Prince Charlie, who thanked her for her hospitality before setting off at a gallop with his small group of men. 'Right,' she said, 'how many men have we here?'

Looking around, she realised the situation she was in. Apart from Lachlan, herself and the women servants most of the Mackintosh were still with the scattered detachments of the Jacobite army. There were only five men of fighting age there at the Hall. Sending the women servants into the nearby woods to hide the Prince's baggage cart which had been left behind, she turned to a man ever after known as *Captein nan coig*, the captain of the five. 'Well, Dairmaid Fraser,' she smiled at the heavy-set middle-aged man before her, 'will you go and see what's coming our way?'

Standing there, a musket in his hand and a sword and pistols in his belt, Fraser bowed his head. 'Och, we might just do a little more than that. Come on lads.'

He turned on his heel, and ran off up the road followed by the other four men, all armed with muskets, pistols and swords.

They ran off on to the moorland, and at a spot on the moor where there was a bit of a hollow about two miles from Moy Hall he stopped and laid his plans. There at *ciste chraig nan eoin*, the rocky hollow of the birds, he spread his men out in a line and told them what to do. They could not hope to halt a force of 1,000 men, but they could delay them, and every minute they held them up the greater was the chance that the Prince might be able to escape.

Minutes later they heard the sound of marching feet. The only other sound they could hear was that of horses' hooves hitting the rough road. By now the rain was falling in torrential bursts as the centre of the storm came nearer. Suddenly there was great flash of lightning and ahead of them on the road the five men saw the approaching troops – all 1,500 of them. At their head, his pipes under his arm and his plaid over his head, strode Donald Ban MacCrimmon, hereditary piper to MacLeod of Dunvegan. Like many of his kin he had hoped that when the clan marched out that it would be to fight for the Young Pretender. And here he was on the side of the British army, marching over the moor to Moy Hall in the midst of a thunderstorm. Again the lightning flashed but this time a shot rang out. MacCrimmon fell, and all at once a volley of fire came from somewhere ahead. Voices shouted, 'To the left, Mackintoshes, and the right, Camerons.' The column halted. Cries of 'Ambush' went up and some of the troops began to turn back. Most of the MacLeods were at the rear of the column and the government men began to fall back on them, causing confusion in the darkness. And all the time the voices up ahead were shouting and shots were ringing out. Loudon, near the head of his troops, was having trouble controlling his horse as men milled around him. Suddenly some of them began to run back towards Inverness! As they ran they prevented the more seasoned troops and the MacLeods from forming up and pressing ahead. Fraser and his men were running across the road ahead, shouting and shooting. It seemed as if there were at least dozens if not hundreds of Jacobites on the road before the government troops. As some of them fled the scene and the others were scattered Loudon tried to rally his troops. Up at the front of the detachment the sound of pipes could be heard. It was Duncan Ban MacCrimmon. Aware he had been mortally wounded he was playing a bright and lively tune that no one had ever heard before. A cousin of his wife crawled up to where he lay and sat beside him while he played his last tune. Several months later the cousin returned to Skye and went to see Donald Ban's widow. He told her of what had happened on that fateful day, and when he mentioned Duncan's last tune, she asked him to sing it. He was no piper, but he could carry a tune, and so he sang it to her and she knew what it was.

'That's the tune he composed when he thought MacLeod was taking them off to fight for the Prince,' she told her cousin. Many years later she said that Duncan had heard the Banshee and knew that his time was short, which was why he had composed the wonderful tune called 'Cha Till MacCruimen', 'Macrimmon No More', that pipers still play today.

Duncan breathed his last, and his pipes groaned into silence while Loudon was still having trouble rallying his men. The increasingly heavy rain, thunder and lightning were spreading confusion – a confusion that was aggravated by the constant whizzing of musket balls coming from the road ahead. With so many of his men streaming back towards Inverness and the rest unable to regroup he gave in and called for a bugler to sound the retreat. Ever since then this skirmish has been known as 'the Rout of Moy' and as the cause of many red faces when the government troops later found out just how many men Captain na Coig had with him that night on the moors near Moy Hall. They had been routed by five men, and the only casualty of the engagement was Donald Ban MacCrimmon.

This was not the last of Colonel Anne's adventures. After the dreadful slaughter of Drummossie Muir, which is known as the battle of Culloden, the MacIntoshes were, like many other Highland clans, at the mercy of the 'Red Army', as the government troops were called. Over 200 MacIntoshes had fallen at Culloden and not long afterward a marauding band of troopers came to Moy Hall. Colonel Anne was there with the local minister when the troops rode up. One of them, noticing the minister looking at his watch, snatched it from his hand.

'Give that back,' said Anne, 'and I will give you a guinea.'

'Damn it, you rebel bitch; you have money, have you?' replied the soldier, grabbing her purse which contained fifty guineas, which was all she had.

'If she has that then she must have more,' shouted another of the English troops as he grabbed her by the shoulders.

'That is all I have left,' said Anne, with all the dignity she could muster.

'Is that right, you rebel whore,' the soldier shouted, and unsheathing his bayonet he stabbed her in the chest. As she fell there was the sound of approaching horses. It was in fact an official party sent to arrest Anne for her part in supporting the Jacobite cause, but the soldiers who arrived first didn't wait to find out. They ran off in the opposite direction with their booty. The horsemen arrived on the scene led by one Sir Everard Faulkner, a minor Scottish laird who knew Colonel Anne. He arrived to find her lying on the ground in the arms of the minister, blood seeping from the wound on her chest. Luckily it was a pretty superficial wound and she managed to tell Faulkner what had happened.

He was about to send some of his men to capture the assailants when Anne stopped him. Realising that if they were captured and court-martialled the influence of Faulkner could easily lead to them being hanged, and even though that might mean she could get her money back, she persuaded Faulkner not to send men after them.

'There has been enough blood shed around here already,' she

said, before being carried in to Moy Hall. When she had recovered she was arrested and for a period of six weeks she was incarcerated at Inverness. However, she was a lady, and was released into the care of the Dowager Lady Mackintosh. Clearly the government representatives in Inverness had no idea of Anne's mother-in-law's role in the Rout of Moy!

After Culloden when the conflict had died down a bit, even if the government felt it necessary to garrison almost the whole of the Scottish Highlands, she returned to lived with Aeneas again at Moy Hall.

A couple of years later they were in London and attended a dance at which the Duke of Cumberland was present. Being told who she was, the Duke asked her to dance with him, having already told the band to play 'Up and Waur them awa' Willie', a well known Hanoverian tune in the Scottish idiom. Colonel Anne graciously consented, but when the tune was finished and the Duke bowed to her she spoke.

'My Lord, would you care for another dance?' she asked. The Duke could hardly refuse, even if this was not quite normal protocol, and nodded his consent.

'Right then,' she said, offering him her hand and, turning towards the band called out: 'Play us "Auld Stewart's back again", lads,' and proceeded into the dance with the furiously blushing Duke of Cumberland.

Fair Annie and the Black Colonel

Over the years much has been made of the Highland clansman's loyalty to his chief. This support was rooted in the ancient traditions of clan life, but it did not apply only to the menfolk. John Farquharson of Inverey was known as 'the Black Colonel', on account of his colouring, not his character. He was made a colonel by Graham of Claverhouse for his actions in fighting on the Royalist side in the years immediately after 1688, when

William and Mary were enthroned after the removal of King Charles II. The Royalist cause was defeated and the Black Colonel was forced to live the life of an outlaw for a while. He was driven from Inverey Castle on several occasions and had to live in caves and other hideouts while the redcoats scoured the countryside for him. While hiding at different times in 'the Colonel's Bed' or 'the Colonel's Cave', both tiny caves over-looking the Ey Burn on the slopes of Carn Mor, he was fed by one of the women of the clan, Annie Ban, or Fair Annie. Every day she brought him food, making sure that she was not seen. It was well known that apart from bringing him his food Annie was warming the Colonel's bed, and that he was in fact much fonder of Annie than he was of his own wife. Although he was an outlaw the government's attempts to capture him were not constant. At times he even felt safe enough to return to his home, Inverey Castle. On one such occasion he was entertaining his good friend, the laird of Daldownie, at Inverey. He was telling his friend of his adventures while 'on the run' from the government troops as they drank claret after their meal. In those far-off days vast amounts of claret were regularly drunk in Scotland and it seems that Inverey and Daldownie were keeping up the custom in great style that night.

That same night an old beggar-woman was sitting outside the inn at Aboyne, about thirty miles down the river from Inverey, when a squadron of dragoons arrived. The old woman wished the officers and the men a good day in English, and in a very gentle voice in Gaelic she wished that their service was in a country as red as their coats and very hot indeed. The officer-in-charge, unaware that the old woman had effectively just told him and his men to go to hell, handed over a few coins to the beggar and the dragoons went into the alehouse. The old woman hung around for a while and even went into the inn herself to purchase a drink. She stood close to the dragoons as she drank. They paid her no attention and she soon overheard that the soldiers were headed for Inverey where they were sure the Black Colonel was in residence.

Now she might have been a travelling woman, and not one of the local Farquharsons, but she was a staunch Jacobite supporter and realised that the Colonel had to be warned. So she slipped away from the inn and headed towards Inverey. Behind her the dragoons billeted themselves on the inn at Aboyne, thus allowing her a good head-start.

All through the evening and the hours of the night the old woman plodded along the banks of the Dee. Her lifetime on the roads and hills of Scotland had made her remarkably fit, and like most women she had considerable powers of stamina. Over Dinnet Moor she went, through the pass of Ballater, and on past Crathie and Braemar. She stopped occasionally for a rest, but never for more than a few minutes at a time, and by the middle of the following day she was nearing Inverey, a considerable feat even in those days when walking long distances was normal for most people. Behind her the troops arose at dawn and after breakfast they set out at a trot towards Inverey. This was before the new roads had been laid and they found some of the going tough. Still, come noon, they too were nearing Inverey.

Back in the castle the Black Colonel and his guest had eventually managed to crawl into their beds, considerably slowed down by the copious amounts of red wine they had drunk. By the time the old woman had reached the castle and convinced the Farquharsons that she had to speak to the Black Colonel himself, the troops were not far behind her. In fact just as the Black Colonel was wakened to hear the old woman's news the dragoons were fording the River Dee just below Inverey.

Farquharson was shaken awake only to hear the news that the 'infidels were at the gate'. Meanwhile his guest was also awakened. Now Daldownie had fallen asleep in his clothes and wasted no time in leaving the castle by the back door and running into the woods. Inverey ran for the castle door, pausing only to pick up a sword and pistol. Out of the castle he ran, and on down to the river. He had wasted no time, and the few people around were treated to the sight of the laird running flat out, naked, through the heather. Because of heavy rain the day before, the river was in spate and Inverey was faced with a raging torrent. With no hesitation as he ran down the hillside the Colonel leapt across the churning waters and disappeared into the woods on the other side. A bridge was later raised in the same spot, which was called 'Drochaid-an-Leum (Bridge of the Leap)'.

Farquharson retreated into the woods by the river and looked back towards Inverey Castle. The dragoons, sure that they had the advantage of surprise, and fired up with the prospect of the reward they had been promised for capturing Farquharson, galloped up to the castle and dismounted. Grabbing a substantial log that was in the grounds for some purpose they rushed furiously with it at the great iron door, or yett, of the Castle. Farquharson of course had left in a bit of hurry and the door was unlocked. So it gave way under the charge of the dragoons and they sprawled in a heap in the entrance hall of Inverey.

The dragoons were sent to search the building, with one of them guarding the door. As they spread out, a tallish figure in a cloak appeared as if from nowhere beside the guard on the door. He was taken by surprise, but he moved to draw his sabre and shouted, 'Surrender or die,' thinking this must be Farquaharson himself. Before he had time to unsheath his blade the dragoon received a heavy thump on the head from a water jug, and as he fell back the cloaked figure muttered '*Gabh an Donas thu,*' the devil take you. The figure moved quickly out of the door and off onto the hillside behind the caslte, but the sentry's challenge had been heard, and soon the officer in charge, a lieutenant, and half a dozen of his men were chasing the cloaked figure.

As ever, the soldiers found running through the heather heavy going, whilst the figure ahead of them seemed to be skipping blithely on. Still the lieutenant had his orders: Inverey was to be taken alive. The intention was to try and hang him as an example to other Jacobite supporters. However though the cloaked figure was moving more easily through the heather than the pursuing redcoats, the distance between them wasn't increasing. In fact, soon the soldiers were beginning to catch up. This spurred on the officer and the half dozen of his fittest men who were keeping up with him, to put on a spurt. At last they came up on the figure, and one of the soldiers threw himself at the fleeing Jacobite. As they tumbled among the heather the hood of the cloak fell away. Expecting to see the black hair of the Colonel the lieutenant was surprised instead to see a head of beautiful long fair hair. The soldier grappling with the figure was pleasantly surprised to find that the body he was holding had rounded curves and softness, unlike the hard musculature of a Highland soldier.

'Take your hands off me, you beast,' came a clearly female voice.

The soldier stood up, and the lieutenant reached forward to pull away the cloak. There lying in the heather was a beautiful young woman, Annie Ban, a wee smile playing around her lips.

'Quick lads, back to the castle,' he shouted, and off they ran. They were of course too late, for John Farquharson had taken advantage of the brief diversion to sneak off up the Ey burn. Daldownie, knowing where he was headed, circled round and they met nine miles further up the burn. When the soldiers realised that the Colonel had eluded their grasp they came back up the hill to seek out Annie Ban. But she too had made herself scarce, and it was a crestfallen group of redcoats who gathered in the courtyard of Inverey Castle to receive their orders.

Furious at what had happened, the redcoat lieutenant decided to set fire to Inverey Castle. Up on the nearby hilltop of Creag a' Chait, Daldownie and Farquharson were watching what was going on. As the flames started to flicker from his ancestral home

Farquharson began to laugh and dance a jig amongst the heather. Daldownie was mystified.

'John, for heaven's sake man. What is up with you? These damned redcoats are firing your home; that is nothing to be celebrating,' he said.

'Ah well, maybe it is, the charter room has half a dozen barrels of black powder [gunpowder] stored in it, and I think they will maybe be getting a little more than they had bargained for,' laughed the Black Colonel. As they watched in anticipation the upper half of the castle burned fiercely, but sadly the fire did not reach the charter room down in the basement.

Whereas a few minutes before Farquharson had been dancing a jig of joy, now he was stamping the ground in a fury, as the castle failed to explode. Soon they were joined on the hill by Annie Ban who had snatched the Colonel's clothes and had had them hidden under her cloak when she diverted the dragoons.

Farquharson then went to one of his caves below the summit of Creag a' Chait. He hadn't seen the redcoat search-party destroyed, but thanks to the old travelling woman he had managed to maintain his freedom. She was well rewarded for her efforts soon after. For several more years the Colonel lived as an outlaw, relying as ever on his faithful Annie Ban.

Annie died when still quite young, and the Colonel was badly affected. After she was buried in the kirkyard at the Chapel of Maidens at Inverey, he composed a lament in Gaelic for her, and when his wife heard about this she was furious. She called on a friend of hers named MacDougall to compose a burlesque of this heartfelt piece. MacDougall actually performed this pastiche in front of Farquharson and included the lines:

> Alas, thou art gone Annie
> Leaving me in deep sorrow
> But never shall thy memory depart
> Until I get butter and barley bread . . .

Barley bread was the traditional bread of the Highlanders, and this was a scathing insult to both the Black Colonel and the memory of his departed love, and to the devotion she had showed him during his time of troubles. Farquharson did not hesitate, but sent out round all the surrounding clachans to bring as much barley bread as could be found. MacDougall was then forced to eat it all at pistol-point. Once he was incapacitated by the amount of food he had eaten, Farquharson had him thrown out of Inverey Castle and the burlesque of his lament was heard no more.

When his own life was drawing to a close the Black Colonel told his family that he wanted to be buried beside Annie Ban at Inverey, but his wife in particular made sure that he was interred in the family burial ground at Castleton, close to Braemar. The funeral was held, and the next morning the Colonel's coffin was found above ground. It was reburied, but the same thing happened. It was reburied a third time, but when it appeared above ground on this third occasion the local people were greatly upset and the Colonel's wife was forced to give in: the Colonel's coffin was taken away and buried beside his Fair Annie.

Such intransigence on the Colonel's part even after death should have been noticed, but quite a few years later, while digging a new grave a pair of gravediggers realised that they had come across the crumbling coffin of the illustrious Black Colonel. For some macabre reason they decided to take a tooth each from the skull as a memento. This they soon regretted, for that very night each man was visited in his bed by the ghost of the Colonel furiously demanding the return of his teeth! Dawn the next morning saw them hurrying from different directions to the Chapel of Maidens kirkyard at Inverey, to replace the missing molars before the new burial was begun.

Mary Cameron

Allan Cameron, of Callart on the north shore of Loch Leven, and his wife had a family of six daughters and two sons. Around the year 1640 a Spanish ship came into the loch. Now this was hardly unknown, but the opportunity to buy fine cloth, clothing and other household goods was rare enough to be very greatly appreciated in most parts of the Highlands. Accordingly, the entire family, with the exception of one daughter, Mary, went on board to see what was on offer. Mary had been locked in her room by one of her brothers as a joke – a fateful decision as it turned out. When the family got on board they soon realised that some of the crew were suffering from the plague. Now we cannot be sure what kind of plague this was, but the horror of such afflictions was such that once people contracted the disease they knew they were doomed. Cameron realised the dreadful fate that had come upon his family and on returning ashore he went home and told Mary not to leave her room no matter what happened. Within a matter of hours her entire family were in the throes of the dreaded sickness and within little more than a day all of them had died. Word of this horror had of course spread like the plague itself, and Donald Cameron from Ballachulish was given the job of coming and setting fire to Allan's house with all the bodies inside, No one would dare even to try to bury plague victims; the only option was to burn down the house around them. On arriving at Callart, Donald was told by a neighbour that Mary was still in the house, still alive, and that she had neither gone to the ship or been in contact with her family: her father had seen to that. Now Donald was a kindly man who knew and liked Mary and was understandably reluctant to see such a bonnie young lass go up in flames with her dead relatives. So he sent word of the situation to young Campbell of Inverawe, the lad whom Mary had been hoping would soon ask her to marry him.

In one of those strange quirks of fate that crop up so often in the Scottish Highlands Campbell was already on his way by boat to Callart. He had had a strange dream that filled him with foreboding. Arriving at the fateful spot he found the house surrounded by a ring of people a good distance from the building, and Donald busy laying brushwood around the building, preparatory to setting fire to it. Campbell did not hesitate, but burst through the ring of people and ran up to the house.

As he approached, Donald Cameron looked up, saw him and stopped what he was doing. Campbell ran round the back of the house and shouted, 'Mary, Mary, it is Diarmaid; climb out of the window and we can get away. Quickly now, Mary, come on.'

The poor lass came to the window and saw her love standing there. Realising that time was of the essence, she immediately climbed out of the window and the pair of them ran into the woods behind the house, away from the gathered crowds. As he half-carried the pale and weakened lass – she had had nothing but water for the three days since the ship had anchored in the Loch – they heard the snap and crackle as the fire began to take hold of the home where her mother and father, brothers and sisters all lay dead. She gave vent to fearful racking sobs as they headed off through the woods. They skirted round all the people who had gathered to watch the house burning and got back to Diarmaid's boat on the shore. From there they set sail back round the coast to his home at Inverawe.

Here though, Diarmaid's father refused to let them into the castle – nobody in their right mind would risk catching the plague. No matter how Diarmaid pleaded through the closed door of his father's house he remained adamant. They would have to go and live in the woods, away from everybody else, till it was clear that they had been spared the dreaded disease.

So the two young lovers lived for the next few weeks in a rough bothy on the slopes of Ben Cruachan, by which time it was clear that neither Mary nor Diarmaid had been infected.

Considering the dreadful situation they had found themselves in, nobody objected to them getting married. In fact, it was agreed all round that the sooner the better. So they were married, but the sadness that seemed to haunt Mary continued. Archie was killed at the Battle of Inverlochy in 1645 and was buried at Ardchattan Priory. Here Mary regularly came to visit her husband's grave, and the laird of Ardchattan, seeing her from the window of his private chapel, fell deeply in love with the beautiful young woman. After a while he declared his love to the grieving widow, and not long afterwards he managed to per-suade her to marry him. Mary, however, could never get Diar-maid out of her mind. Not only had she loved him, but he had shown great courage as well as love when he had come to the plague-infested house at Callart to rescue her. Mary's sadness eventually ended when she died on the eve of her marriage to Ardchattan, and no one had any doubt that she had died of a broken heart. Ever since that time there have been occasional sightings of a ghostly figure, known as the Green Lady of Inverawe, in the rooms of the mansion that was built to replace the old castle.

Morag of the Heads

On a small islet off the island of Vatersay there is an ancient graveyard which contains the remains of a woman who was known as Morag of the Heads. She was the daughter of the laird and she became famous for her dietary habits. Morag had a very high opinion of herself and had been indulged ever since child-hood; she had grown up with the habit of eating her favourite food, ox-tongue, every day. It is likely that MacNeill of Barra did not know this when he asked for her hand, but he certainly knew about it afterwards! Every day a beast had to be killed so that MacNeill's wife could have her favourite dish, and this soon had serious effect on his wealth. For many centuries the Highlanders and islanders had counted wealth in cattle, for they provide the most moveable and obvious form of exchange apart from their importance as a food source. It was this importance that no doubt lay behind the well-attested clan habit of raiding other clans to 'lift' their cattle.

Now although clan chiefs were great ones for showing off their wealth, both in cattle and in personal possessions, this was due to their status as heads of their kin group, rather than as rich men in their own right, and the constant depletion of MacNeill's stock was likely to lead to hard times for many in the clan. It was, after all, the chief's duty to look after the poor, the sick and those unable to provide for themselves. However, like most chiefs, and truth to tell, like most Gaels of his time, MacNeill of Barra was a proud man and he did not wish to complain directly to his young wife about her indulgence. He thought this would make him look small in her eyes. Nevertheless, something just had to be done.

It so happened that when he hit upon the solution he and Morag were staying at Eoligarry in the north of Barra. He sent word to the chief herdsman to go round the island and gather up 365 cattle from the islanders. The herdsman was simply to explain that the chief was borrowing them for a short while, an explanation being necessary for removing people's own beasts. As the great herd came into the fields below Eoligarry they made a lot of noise and Morag went to the window to look.

'Och,' she said, 'is that not a magnificent sight, all those fine head of cattle?' 'Well, aye it is,' replied the chief in a diffident manner, 'but what would you think of someone whose singular appetite would be responsible for the slaughter of that entire herd in a single year?'

'Now that would be . . .' Morag began, but stopped. She turned and looked at her husband, realising exactly what lesson he was trying to teach her. She nodded, blushed and smiled, and from that time onwards she still ate well but was never profligate again. And when she did have ox-tongue she appreciated it all the more.

However, this event may have affected how MacNeill saw his wife. She died before her husband, and during her final illness she asked that she be buried somewhere in sight of her native Coll. Accordingly, when she passed away MacNeill arranged for a boat to carry her body from Eoligarry to the tiny islet of Uinessan. It was a misty, hazy sort of day when Morag was taken to her final resting place, and not till the following day was it realised that the view to Coll from Uinessan was blocked by the hill on the island of Muldonaich. In their respect for her the clansfolk would have been glad to dig her up and move her somewhere else in fulfilment of her last request. But MacNeill himself had other ideas, and said that she should rest where she was, as she had caused him enough bother while she was alive, without tormenting him further now she was dead.

The Old Woman of Moy

Back at the end of the eighth century Adomnan, Abbot of Iona and biographer of Columba, passed a law called the Cain Adomnan. This was intended to secure the status of women as non-combatants, and many people have suggested that it meant that before this time it was possible, if not normal, for women in the British Isles to go into battle. The great queen of the Iceni, Boudicca, is a well-known example of the female British warrior, and some of the oldest tales from these islands refer to other women both as warriors and as teachers of warriors. It would be silly to think that there would be such fierce women down south while our own would be gentle and self-effacing creatures, no? In ancient traditions from Britain and Ireland there are several examples of famous warriors being given arms and armaments by women, sometimes after being trained in their use by these women themselves. Probably the best known of these was the great Irish hero Cu Chulain, who was sent for training in arms by the great female warrior

Scathach, on an island off Scotland's east coast. It therefore seems clear that in ancient tribal Britain the idea of the Amazon or female warrior was not that unusual. However, after the enactment of the Cain Adomnan it seems that female warriors were no longer to be feared.

But the clan system of medieval Scotland had its roots far back in the distant past and it seems that the idea of the female warrior was not entirely forgotten. After the rout of the MacDonalds at Blar-na-pairc in or around 1489 a considerable group of their warriors headed south from the carnage of the battlefield. They had to cross the River Conan and chose to do it near Moy. The river was running high, and being strangers to the area they did not know where it was safe to try and ford the river.

Near the banks of the river they came across an old woman who lived nearby. Intent as they were with getting as far away from the rampaging MacKenzies as quickly as possible, the men gave no thought to their actions on the way north. Their sole concern was crossing the river and heading home.

'Good day, mother,' one of them said to the old woman as they approached, while many of the others kept looking over their shoulders for pursuit, 'can you please tell us where it is safe to ford this river?'

The old woman looked at him and smiled. She knew fine what had happened at the church at Contin, where so many perished in the flames. 'Ah well,' she said, 'it is a fierce river right enough, but if you go upstream just a few hundred yards there is a wide straight stretch of the river where it looks really black and deadly, but there is hardly any depth to it at all.' At once the MacDonalds headed off at a good pace – some say they were in their hundreds – and coming to the aforesaid stretch of the river they all plunged in, keeping close together.

But the sure footing they expected was not there to be found. Some of them were swept away by the sheer force of the stream at once, and were drowned, while others managed to get to the banks and cling on to bushes and tree branches overgrowing the water. But such was the inexorable power of the River Conan at that point that none of them could pull themselves up without breaking the bushes and branches they clung to. Any who tried simply lost their grip and were swept away like their comrades. As they hung there the man who had first spoken to the old woman saw her and a group of other women approaching the banks of the river.

'Ah, help us now, mother, we are in dreadful danger here,' he cried.

As the women came closer he saw that each one of them carried a sickle, the short curved-bladed reaping tool of the Highlands. On they came and without a word they began to cut through the bushes and branches the invaders were clinging to. One by one they were swept away down the river and any man who looked as though he might be able to pull himself up onto the banks found that he grasped at nothing that could help him as the women wielded their sickles. Each time the first old woman swung her sharp-edged tool she repeated the same phrase.

'Well, as you have taken so much already you might as well take that also!' And as she spoke her sickle did its deadly work. Soon the last of the invading clansmen had been drowned or swept off down river and quiet returned to the strath. The women turned and went home to put away their sickles till they would be needed for more normal work. In honour of that day's good work at the riverbank the sickle itself was long after known in the area as the Old Woman of Moy, in honour of the old lady and her companions.

MacLaine and the Ugly Woman

Back in the sixteenth century on the island of Mull relations between the MacLeans of Duart and the MacLaines of

Lochbuie tended to be somewhat variable. Both branches claimed descent from a common ancestor, Gillean of the Battle-axe, a renowned warrior in the time of Alexander III. Now at one time in the sixteenth century the chief of the Lochbuie clan was Old John, the Toothless, who was their eighth chief, and he had been having a lot of trouble with his son Ewan, a proud and ambitious young man. In fact he was so ambitious he wanted to take over the chieftainship of the clan from his father. Open warfare broke out between the two, with Ewan finding some support among the younger warriors. On his way into another battle with his father in 1538 Ewan is said to have met the Washer at the Ford. Now this was a well-known form of banshee or female spirit whose speciality was to foretell death in battle by washing bloody clothes in a river. Any who saw her were doomed to die. After seeing her Ewan's time was up and sure enough in the ensuing battle he was beheaded by one of his father's men. Old John had seen off his ambitious son, but at a terrible price. Not only did he have no heir, but in his battle with Ewan he had called for the assistance of the MacLeans of Duart, under their chief Hector. The MacLaines lost a great many men on both sides of the battle, leaving them almost powerless, and it was now a pretty simple matter for Hector to take over the lands of Lochbuie, which he had long coveted. However, he could not bring himself to have Old John killed, since he liked the old man.

So he decided to send him to a form of internal banishment. As luck would have it, there was an ideal location to hand. This was the small island of Carn na Burgh Mor, one of the little group of Treshnish Islands between Mull and Tiree. There was a small castle there with just enough land to support a few cows and grow some barley and vegetables. Before sending Old John there Hector said, 'Well, is there any request you have before we send you to the island, John?'

'Well, if it is all right by you, Hector,' John replied sarcastically, 'I wouldn't mind having a woman to cook and to clean for me. It is not the sort of thing I am used to doing myself.'

Hector realised that there was some sense in this, but his first thought was that John, though he was a fair age, would probably try to father a new heir with any woman he was sharing his island retreat with. So keeping John under lock and key for the time being, he sent word around the area that he needed the services of the ugliest woman to be found, and that whichever woman was chosen her kin would receive the blessings of the chief and a few goodies besides. Now this was a strange request, and though people generally responded well to their chief's wishes, this was very unusual. Highland society functioned through a series of close-knit communities, and it was a terrible thing to be claiming that a kinswoman was the ugliest female around, both for the woman concerned and for her immediate family. Nevertheless the request was from the chief, and there was always benefit in having done the chief a favour, apart from the inducements that were on offer.

So within a short while a few candidates were found. We have no record of how Hector chose the woman but one was chosen to accompany MacLaine to the island. Perhaps on account of her appearance, the woman concerned had never found a husband, and though she looked old she was in fact relatively young, and was certainly of child-bearing age. However, Hector considered her so repulsive that he had no doubt that John would never approach her in any sexual sense. So the pair of them were sent off to Carn na Brugh More, and for a few years things seemed to be going smoothly, with no trouble whatever for Hector. But it has long been understood that beauty is only skin deep, and that there is more between a man and a woman than how they look. Also, the needs of the physical body have a way of becoming quite irresistible. So it came to pass that one spring the MacLean clansmen taking supplies to the island noticed that the woman was unmistakably pregnant.

When he heard of this, Hector flew into a rage and immediately ordered the woman to be brought ashore. She was allowed to go back to her home and family provided she was accompanied by a midwife and a clansmen who had strict instructions to kill any male baby at birth. Hector was set on making sure his acquisition of the Lochbuie lands would become permanent. No way was he going to allow the possibility of some descendant of Old John the Toothless turning up in subsequent years to lay claim to them. At last the time of the birth grew near, and, when the child that came into the world was seen to be a girl, the midwife and her companion went off, with a great sense of relief, to tell Hector that a girl had been born. They were not long gone however, when, almost an hour after his sister, a twin boy came on the scene. The woman's family realised they had to act quickly and the wee boy was bundled off in the care of a MacLaine who had seven sons of his own. Initially the boy was brought up in a cave somewhere on the slopes of Beinn Mhor, well away from prying eyes. Somehow, maybe it was some MacLaine boasting abut the fertility of his aged and imprisoned chief after one whisky too many, word of the birth of the son came to Hector's ears. At once he sent a large force of his own men to the lands around Lochbuie to search for the child, and at the same time he let it be known there would be a considerable reward for any information about him. Now clan ties were incredibly strong, but there are always those whose greed will overcome any sense of decency or propriety, and somebody let slip the name of the place where the child had been taken after his birth. By now it was summer, and the seven sons of William MacLaine were up at the sheilings with the cattle. This was part of the ancient system of transhumance when the young people of a clan or tribe would take cattle up into the lush summer pastures of the Highlands to fatten them, while leaving the crops to grow back at the clachans lower down, where the older people remained. William was taken prisoner by Hector's men at the clachan and led up to the shielings, his arms tied behind his back. There he was asked where the child was and refused to answer.

As his seven sons came back to the shieling, one after another, they too were questioned. All refused to speak. So one after another, on Hector's orders, the MacLeans beheaded the lads in front of their father. When the last one was killed, the leader of the MacLeans asked, 'Well, what do you think now then, old man?'

'Well at least I can die happy,' he replied with a grim smile, 'knowing that my sons were loyal to the end.'

This infuriated the Macleans, who killed him on the spot, thus ensuring they would never know where the missing child was. He had in fact been sent to the very edge of the MacLaine lands to live with another family. Old John lived on in his isolation, and when he eventually died at a very advanced age his son, Murdoch Gearr [Short], was about fifteen years old. He was a small lad, but strong and quick, and had been well taught in the ways of Highland weapons and warfare. One day, soon after his sixteenth birthday, he was visited by a woman he had never seen before.

This was his mother, who had come to tell him that he was in fact the hereditary chief of the Lochbuie MacLaines and that it might be best if he left the country for a while. Although Murdoch had never seen his natural mother before, he had long suspected that there was something that made him different from other lads. His foster bothers and the other young men of the clachan had always made a point of looking out for him, and though they never bowed the knee to him, he had long realised that they held in him in some regard. He had simply been told that he was an orphan and that his mother had died in childbirth. Little was said of his father other than that he had been a great warrior in his time and close to the old chief. Now all was clear, and he realised that his companions and their families expected him to reclaim the Lochbuie lands for the MacLaines. None of the Maclaines had ever accepted the overlordship of MacLean of Duart and they were all looking forward to the day when they would have their own chief again. Now Murdoch was a bright lad and loved his foster family dearly, but once he realised that he was the hereditary chief of the MacLaines he knew that his path was laid out for him.

There was little doubt that a spell away from Lochbuie was a good idea, so he sailed off to Ireland on a passing trading ship, taking a dozen of his foster brothers and close friends with him. Most of them were already experienced warriors, and while in Ireland they would concentrate on further developing his skills as a warrior.

So he went to Ireland, where, the story tells us, he remained for a year and a day developing his fighting abilities and laying his plans. Whatever the length of time it was – and it was probably a bit longer than a year and a day – by the time he returned he had his plans well laid. With the advantage of surprise he gathered up a band of MacLaines who had been awaiting his return and made a frontal assault on Lochbuie Castle. The attack was short, sharp and successful, and those followers of MacLean of Duart who weren't killed were driven off from Lochbuie. And once he was secure in his ancestral home Murdoch Gearr spent many an evening looking out over the slopes of Beinnna Croise and the waters of Loch Buie, thinking how well things had worked out according to the wishes of the father he had never known.

Man's Inhumanity to Man

The Smooring of the MacDonalds

One time in 1577 a group of MacLeods landed on Eigg, populated by members of the MacDonald clan. Now feelings between the clans often ran high, and clansmen would often act towards members of other clans in ways they would never even contemplate towards their own relatives. On this visit it seems that the MacLeods insulted some of the MacDonald women. Young men at any time can be loutish, but in this case, whether it was no more than that, or whether one of them had dared to lay a hand on one of the island women is unclear. What is clear though is that the MacDonalds were having none of this kind of behaviour from a bunch of unruly MacLeods.

Word swiftly went round the area and armed men immediately flocked to where the incomers were. All the island people had long been used to raids and had been raised to respond quickly to dangerous situations. The MacLeods found themselves surrounded and captured without a chance of even drawing their weapons. They were securely tied up and taken to the shore, where they were thrown into the birlinn that had brought them there. The MacDonalds then towed them out to sea with one of their own boats, and once they were a good way off the shore they cast the MacLeods adrift. The MacLeods thought that their end had come, especially as a strong wind began to blow. The waters off the west coast of Scotland, though occasionally calm and as flat as glass, were full of ever-changing

135

currents and tides, and it required a fair level of seamanship to sail around as freely as the locals had been doing for centuries, if not millennia. In fact seamanship was pretty much taken for granted, but in a boat helplessly bobbing up and down on the waters the MacDonalds knew they were in extreme danger. A sudden squall could easily erupt and tip the boat over. They realised the people of Eigg had been very clever; if their boat was swamped and they drowned it would be thought back on Skye that they had simply gone down in bad weather. Their deaths would seem like an accident.

One of them, however, despite the rocking motion of the boat, managed to pull himself up and look over the gunwale. Despite the bobbing up and down he realised that the wind was blowing them back towards Skye.

'We might be all right lads,' he shouted to his companions, 'the wind is blowing us back to Skye.'

At this they all began to hope that they might survive, and a few hours later the birlinn beached on Skye. They managed to roll themselves out of the boat and onto the beach, where they were found by some of their clansmen a few hours later. All they were suffering from was cold and a few cuts and bruises. Well, that was all they were suffering from physically. When they had to tell their kin what had happened they were all ashamed that their unacceptable behaviour had led to them having such a close call with death. They were forgiven the fact that they had not managed to put up a fight, but when the MacLeod heard about what had happened he was furious.

He was furious at the lads who had gone to Eigg, but most of his anger was directed at the MacDonalds on Eigg. What they had done was a dreadful insult to his clan, no matter how the young lads had behaved, and he set his heart on revenge. He didn't hesitate, and at once he sent *crann tara*, the fiery cross, around the district. This was a simple but very effective tool for gathering the fighting men of the clan. A large cross was made of wood, with one end of the cross-piece dipped in goat's blood, and the other scorched in a fire. One, or sometimes two warriors, if the cross was large enough, would set out for the nearest clachan, running as fast as possible, holding up the *crann-tara*, and regularly shouting out the clan's slogan or battle cry. As soon as any man saw the cross or heard the slogan, he would stop what he was doing, head home for his weapons on the run, and make for the clan-gathering spot with all speed. Whenever a runner tired he would be replaced by another clansman and the cross would circulate round every clachan and glen in the clan's lands. Within a matter of hours the MacLeod had gathered several hundred armed men together. The MacLeod had spent the intervening time organising enough birlinns for them all to head for Eigg.

On Eigg the first that the people knew of the approaching fleet was when a young lad who had been out on the cliffs hunting birds came running into Kildonan shouting, 'The MacLeods are coming; the MacLeods are coming.' Word was sent round all the clachans immediately, and realising that there were far too many warriors approaching to make fighting a viable idea the entire population headed south to the great cave known as Uamh Fraing [Francis's Cave]. This great cave had a tiny entrance, part-hidden by a waterfall, and was virtually impossible for a stranger to find. The MacDonalds of Eigg were all sworn to keep its precise location a secret from any non-islander, and the cave had saved many lives in previous centuries. Soon every living human in the island was safely hidden in the cave. They had all had brought food and water and were content to hide out till the MacLeods got frustrated and left.

The MacLeods arrived and scoured the island. There was no sign of any of the inhabitants. The MacLeods realised that they could not have left the island; their boats were all on the shore, so they realised they had to have some kind of hideaway. Rumours of just such a place were known throughout the Hebrides, but no non-islander had ever found out exactly where the hideout was. MacLeod was intent on having his revenge though, and, rather than go back to Skye he decided to stay on Eigg for a while to see what would develop. He posted lookouts on all the high points of the island and settled down with his men at the deserted village of Kildonan, helping themselves to whatever food and drink they needed. Two days later the word came that a MacDonald had been spotted in the south. One of the MacLeod lookouts had seen him spying out the land from a hillside and had duly followed him at a distance till he saw him disappear into Uamh Fraing.

At once the entire MacLeod force headed to the cave. Once there, MacLeod himself called for the inhabitants to come out. They had no intention of doing that. It was obvious to the Skyemen that they could not fight their way in to the cave and the MacDonalds thought they would just sit there till MacLeod gave up in frustration. And they were not slow to let MacLeod know that that was what they had intended doing. They did not realise how furious the Macleod had become; firstly, at the original insult, and then at being thwarted by the MacDonalds evading him and lastly, at the catcalls coming from inside the cave. So he did a dreadful thing. He got some his men to go and gather brushwood, while another group were sent to the cliff-top above to divert the stream away from the entrance. The Skyemen then heaped piles of brushwood and driftwood against the entrance to the cave and set it on fire. Inside the MacDonalds never had a chance. All of the 395 men, women and children were smothered to death with the smoke from MacLeod's fire.

And Blood Shall Lead to Blood

Amongst the clans of Scotland the addiction to battle frequently led to feuds that resulted in dreadful slaughter. For reasons of their own, clans often got involved in Scotland's political and religious disputes. Although such involvement could arise from deeply felt religious beliefs, on many occasions down the centuries it was more often in order to try and gain land or gather booty on raids, or sometimes simply to settle old scores. Now James Lamont, 14th chief of the clan who originated in the Cowal peninsula, supported King Charles in the bitter religious disputes from the 1630s onwards. This could not fail to bring him into direct conflict with the head of the Campbells, the Earl of Argyll, and by far the most powerful chief in the area. Now Lamont was married to the daughter of Colin Campbell of Ardkinglas, the Earl's cousin, and was warned directly by Argyll not to take the field against the Protestant cause. In 1645 he was given the King's Commission, but family pressure prevailed and somehow he was persuaded to join Argyll against the Royalist forces under Montrose.

Now in the early months of 1645 the Marquis of Montrose and his troops were wintering at Inveraray, the very heartland of the Campbell possessions. Knowing that an army would oppose them, Montrose decided to advance towards Loch Ness. While on the road, scouts came to report that a large band of Campbells and some government troops, over 3,000 men in total, were in and around Inverlochy, just outside Fort William. They were strengthening the defences of the castle as well as harrying the lands of the Cameron, MacDonald and Stewart clans in the area, all of whom were supporters of the Royalist cause at that time.

Now John Graham, The Marquis of Montrose, was never a man to flinch from combat, and he wanted to find out exactly what the government forces were up to. With the assistance of men from the Clan Cameron who took his force along little-known paths, Montrose's force came around the side of Ben Nevis till they were overlooking the fort at Inverlochy, which was surrounded by the Campbells and government troops. The troops at Inverlochy saw some of them up on the shoulder of the mountain, but it was assumed that this was a small raiding party and they were ignored. Argyll, who was personally in command at Inverlochy, knew that Montrose had a far smaller force than he had and also felt pretty safe. An attack, even from Montrose, seemed to be beyond any possibility. At this point Montrose took advantage of the Highlanders' basic hardiness. All night long, in freezing temperatures, the Royalists lay wrapped in their plaids awaiting the dawn. It seems likely that many of them would have used the old Highland trick of soaking their plaids in water before lying on the ground wrapped up in them. As wool's insulating properties are increased when it gets wet, this seeming insanity was in fact a very sensible and clever thing to do.

Down in the Covenanting camp Argyll was so unconcerned by the presence of what he thought was a small party of the enemy that he left Inverlochy to attend to matters elsewhere, and passed the command to General Baillie the same night. However, come the morning Montrose brought all of his troops on to the skyline and Billie realised that he was facing the entire Royalist army. Still he knew that he outnumbered Montrose by nearly two to one. By the deployment of Montrose's men it was obvious they were set for battle, so the Government troops lined up for the fray.

They lined up along a ridge of firm ground that ran from north to south, with about 500 seasoned Lowland troops on either flank. The centre of the government line was taken by the fighting men of the Clan Campbell, armed with a variety of weapons, guns and swords, and the axes still favoured by many Highland warriors. Their left flank was close to the old castle and Campbell of Auchinbreck placed a group of about fifty musketeers here to cover the left flank. However, there was a problem that none of the officers took note of: the way that they had their men lined up so that they were very close to each other. Now Highland warriors liked room to fight, and the Royalists on the slopes above began to think that a charge against such a closely packed group would be very effective, and their officers had trouble in keeping them from pouring down the hill at the enemy.

The delay, however, was only a short one, and soon Montrose's men came thundering down the hill in the traditional Highland charge. This was a form of attack that had long been practised amongst the Highland clans. It was simple. Men would run at speed down the hill and use their impetus to smash through whatever opposition lay in front of them. With the sharp iron spike in the centre of the targe held firmly to their left forearms and the short basket-hilted swords in their right hands the charging warriors came at their foes with two weapons. The targes could catch swords, bayonets or even pikes, and these could be turned, leaving the opposition fighter exposed to a sword blow. There was yet another aspect to this simple attack. Each man held his dirk, more like a short sword than a knife, in his left hand and could bring it into play as well. The combination of the impetus of the charge and the weapons in the hands of men who had been trained to use them since childhood made the Highland charge a ferocious event, even after firearms had become relatively common. Muskets, the original firearms, had only one shot, and before they could be reloaded it was normal for the Highland charge to be amongst opposition troops hacking and slashing. At close quarters there was no finer fighting man than the Highland warrior, and well into the eighteenth century the Highland charge was almost irresistible. It depended of course on controlling the high ground, but that day at Inverlochy Montrose's men had that control.

When the charge hit the government line was smashed and those in front were driven back on the rest of the troops behind them, making them effectively irrelevant in the battle. Even experienced troops who had fought in many battles in England and abroad were horrified at the slaughter that was taking place as their comrades fled all round them. The force of the charge turned the left flank of the government troops and forced them back into the rest of their men in the centre. Their lines crumbled. Some of them tried to reach the castle to get shelter, but were cut off by the Royalist troops under Sir Thomas Ogilvie and were cut down as they fled for safety.

In the centre the Campbell warriors were too tightly packed to allow the fleeing front line through, and could only watch helplessly as their kin died before their eyes. Capable and brave warriors as many of them were, they could only slow the charge, not halt it, and within minutes the Royalists had broken right through to capture the government's standard. Now this was always a significant turning point in any battle, and as the standard was taken by Montrose's men, many of the surviving Campbells scattered and ran. The officers had deployed them badly, and with so many of their kin having paid the price already there was little doubt that discretion was now the better par of valour. The small remaining pockets of resistance were soon mopped up by the Royalist army. As the government troops fled the field they were pursued by their foes and it has long been said that the slaughter continued on the run for more than ten miles as the scattered clansmen headed towards Lochaber.

The effectiveness of the charge can be seen in the figures. It has been calculated that about 1,500 men of Argyll's command died that day, and only eight of the Royalists! Sadly one of that eight was Sir Thomas Ogilvie, who had fought so well. Still, death in battle was something no true warrior feared. This was a major victory for the Stewart cause, and as a result of it troops had to be sent up from England.

Not all of the government men who failed to escape were cut down; some were captured, and James Lamont was one of them. He was given the option of joining the Royalist cause immediately after the battle and he gladly accepted. He had never wanted to fight against the forces of the man he considered to be his true king anyway. So he became an officer in the Royalist army.

From this time through to the last gasp of the Jacobites in the late 1750s there were many instances of people being drawn one way by political and religious beliefs and the other way by family ties and kinship loyalties. Like many of the clan chiefs in the west, Lamont had for long greatly resented the expanding powers of the Campbells under the Earl of Argyll. Despite being related to him by marriage, Lamont saw an opportunity to attack the power of the Campbells who were, from his point of view, rebels against the legitimate king. This way he hoped to regain some of the ancestral lands that had been lost to the Campbells in earlier years, and thus to strengthen his own clan. What today might seem to us to be little more than opportunism was, for many, no more than following the habits of a lifetime and many centuries of tradition in putting the interests of their kin first.

Lamont was soon leading a considerable force of MacDonalds and MacDonnells whose feuding with the Campbells is a recurrent theme throughout much of Scotland's history. Where once the MacDonalds had possessed the Lordship of the Isles and were powerful enough to rival kings, the Earl of Argyll was now the most powerful chief in all Scotland and all of the branches of the MacDonalds resented this.

As ever, when Highlanders were involved in battle the lifting of cattle and other moveable goods was an intrinsic part of their activities and they harried the Argyll lands, going so far as to raid the castle at Ardkinglas, Lamont's father-in-law's home! Now war at any time is a fearful business, and dreadful things happen when men are driven by the combination of excitement, fear and expectation all at the same time. Even though no Highland warrior would ever admit to feeling fear, they were human. Still, there can be no excuse for barbarity.

Lamont's force headed down towards Cowal, and coming to

Strachuir they found that a group of about thirty Campbell troops had been given shelter there. It was likely that some of them were related by marriage to the people there, but this meant nothing to the Royalists. The Campbell clansmen were slaughtered out of hand and a fair number of the local residents along with them; they paid dearly for sticking to the traditions of Highland hospitality. However, the blood was up and the whole of Glen Branter was looted by Lamont's men. Many of the inhabitants fled into the hills, but there were instances of old and frail people being driven out of their homes to die of exposure. Lamont didn't have it all his own way though, and was met in battle by a force of Campbells on the slopes of Cnoc Mhadaidh, overlooking the Holy Loch. After routing this force the Royalists came down to the shores of the loch to lay siege to the old stronghold of Kilmun Castle, which was held by the Campbells.

In the harrying of the Campbell regions of Cowal, James's brother Archibald was well to the fore with a band of Irish warriors under the leadership of Montrose's famous lieutenant Colkitto. The siege of Kilmun Castle itself was brought to an end by a promise of quarter to the inhabitants, but when they came out of their stronghold they were tied up, taken up the lochside and slaughtered. Civil War anywhere is a brutal business and there is no doubt that there were all too many acts of extreme barbarity committed on both sides. The Royalists then went south to attack Dunoon, another Campbell holding.

After this horrific event Lamont returned to his home at Toward Castle and it wasn't long after this that Montrose died, which effectively put an end to the Royalist resistance in Scotland. The Campbells' position of power grew even stronger. And there was no possibility that the events at Kilmun and Dunoon would be forgotten. The following year Campbell of Ardkinglas personally led an attack on Lamont in Toward Castle. It soon became clear that the Campbells were ready to lay siege to the castle for as long as it took to starve Lamont and his people out.

Now Ardkinglas was of course James's father-in-law, and no doubt James thought that he could turn this fact to his advantage. Somehow he managed to get Ardkinglas to come close to the battlements of the old castle and they had a short discussion. The effect of this was that James was convinced it was safe to bring out his people from the castle – they had the word of his wife's father that they would not be harmed. But the cost of the massacre at Kilmun would have to be paid at some point.

The Lamonts were rounded up by the Campbells and forced to watch as the ancient stronghold was reduced to rubble before their eyes. The Campbells then destroyed many of the houses round about, lifting everything of value that was in them. After this the Lamonts were escorted to Ascog Castle, where another group of the Lamonts had taken refuge, and were also being besieged by Campbell troops. On being told that both he and his people would be spared by Ardkinglas, James called on his kin at Ascog to surrender to the Campbells. Once they had left the security of the old fort the Campbells proceeded to destroy the building, just as they had done at Toward Point. Cleary Ardkinglas, under the instructions of the Earl of Argyll himself, was making sure that the power of the Lamonts in Cowal was to be ended.

Once both castles had been destroyed the whole of the assembled Lamonts – men, women and children – were herded off to Dunoon Castle where they were packed into the dungeon. Here they were kept in atrocious conditions for eight long days. Then they were led out of their imprisonment. It is easy to imagine the relief they felt at reaching the fresh air, but it was a relief that did not last long. We know from records of the time that the Campbells proceeded to kill almost every one of their captives, many of them having their throats slit. Neither women nor children were spared this dreadful slaughter and thirty-six of the most prominent men of the Lamonts, the close relatives of James himself, were hung from a great ash tree nearby. Many of them were cut down while still breathing and then flung onto the heaped bodies of their kinfolk in great pits that had been previously dug. Some of them struggled to get out of the pits but were thrown back and the earth heaped upon them. A contemporary report refers to the Lamonts being 'most cruelly, traitorously, and perfidiously, murthered, without assys or order of law'. Truly, it was a horrible act of revenge. So horrible in fact that the Provost of Dunoon objected so furiously at the shameless slaughter of women and children that he too had his throat slit and was thrown into a pit.

For James, though, the horror continued. After being forced to witness the wholesale slaughter of so many of his clan he and Archibald were taken to Dunstaffnage Caslte by Campbell and thrown into the dungeon there. Perhaps Ardkinglas was reluctant to kill his daughter's husband or perhaps he simply wanted to prolong his agony. Whatever the cause, for the next five years James Lamont and his brother festered in the squalor of the dungeon of Dunstaffnage before James died. The power of the Lamont clan had been broken, and the Campbells had had their revenge.

However, the only constant in life is change, and in 1660 King Charles II came to the thrones of England and Scotland in what is known as the Restoration. The Campbells were the new king's sworn enemies, and Sir Colin Campbell was captured and tried for treason to the king. At his trial the details of the dreadful slaughter at Dunoon were presented, along with other charges, and in 1661 Sir Colin Campbell was beheaded for treason. But that was of no solace to the Lamonts.

The story is told that such was the horror of the event that the great ash tree that served as a scaffold at Dunoon shed its leaves that very day in June and died. And so it stood leafless and lifeless for two more years. When at last it was cut down the roots seeped a substance like blood! It was as if streams of blood were running from the roots of the tree, and a few years further on the

146

roots themselves were dug up by local people and fresh soil brought in to fill in the holes. This put an end to the seeping blood, but it is said as long as there are Lamonts alive the history of that dreadful slaughter will never be forgotten.

The Slave Ship

Now traditionally the loyalty of the clansmen to their chief was absolute. The chief represented the whole clan dealings with other kin-groups and was the dispenser of justice amongst his own people. However, human nature is such that there are always those who see no value in loyalty to anyone in the face of personal advantage. Down the centuries there were instances where chiefs were removed, or even killed, for effectively breaking the trust of the clan. However, in the latter years of the clan system, as the new money economy began to seem attractive, there were some chiefs whose behaviour towards their own people was such that it almost beggars belief.

As the traditional Highland way of life changed, the old practice of holding land *a' ghlaive* – by the sword on behalf of the whole clan – was replaced by written charters. And these written charters said that the chiefs owned the land, not the clan. Sadly, most of the chiefs seem to have accepted this major shift in the economic, social and sociological structure of Highland society without a murmur. Where once the chief was the leader of his people, now he was no different from an English landlord, and, as with landlords everywhere, loyalty to his tenants was of no economic benefit whatsoever. The tragic circumstances of the Highland Clearances – following the even more widespread earlier clearances of the cottars from the Lowlands – have been well documented, but there is one instance of despicable behaviour that stands out even amongst those black tales.

In the 1730s Alexander MacDonald of Sleat was the chief of the Skye MacDonalds and his sister was married to Norman

MacLeod of Dunvegan. Both of these characters laid claim to illustrious pedigrees and considered themselves men of some standing.

In September 1739 the *William*, a ship registered in Ireland, dropped anchor in Loch Bracadale, a few miles south of Dunvegan Castle. The captain was one William Davidson and to all intents and purposes this was just another visiting trading-ship. Appearances however, can often be deceptive, and the *William* had in fact been chartered by MacDonald of Sleat and MacLeod of Dunvegan as part of a truly sinister plan. Another MacLeod, Norman, from the Isle of Harris, was acting as their agent in a plan which, simply put, was to sell a shipload of MacLeods and MacDonalds as slaves. The American and West Indian plantation owners were crying out for slaves; they would pay a good price, and the two clan chiefs, long rid of any feelings towards their own kinfolk, were driven by nothing other than greed for gold. The plan was simple: if anyone found out what they were doing or raised any questions, it would be simple to say that the clansfolk on board the ship had all been found guilty of various crimes and their sentence had been transportation.

By now many of the people on Harris had been turned into little more than serfs, forced to work for MacLeod for pitiful wages. In a premonition of much more of the same to come, they had been turned away from their traditional lands where they, like their predecessors, had followed an ancient lifestyle where self-sufficiency had been the norm for hundreds if not thousands of years. Now though, they were effectively surplus to the requirements of their landlord, whose role as their chief meant so little to him. Just as countless others did in subsequent years, Norman MacLeod was responsible for breaking the ancient links to the land by constantly raising the tenants' rents and clearing land for incoming flocks of sheep. The lands that had been held for generations by the warriors of the clan under the leadership of their chief were now no more than the private possessions of a wealth-obsessed laird.

When the *William* arrived in Bloch Bracadale the locals were pleased to welcome the crew when they came ashore. The old tradition of Highland hospitality had not been forgotten, despite the people being impoverished, and the crew were invited into local homes and to share whatever food the people had. This had been reckoned on, and quite cynically the crew members then invited the families with whom they had shared bread to come and look over the ship. This was an unusual treat for the local people, a highlight in their increasingly drab and hard lives, and group after group came aboard. Once they were on board however, their genial hosts soon showed their true colours as men, women and children were quickly grabbed, gagged and tied up before being sent down to the lower decks. As this was going on other families were approaching the ship in boats. By the time the vessel sailed there were more than sixty captives in the hold.

The plan had worked a treat, and the ship then called at Finsbay on Harris and at Loch Portan on Lewis, where the same procedure was faithfully followed. The local people had no idea what was going on, and the crew of the *William* had no trouble in going about their nefarious business. After the third landfall the *William* had amassed a total of 111 captives on board, and this was reckoned to be enough. From Lewis the *William* set sail for its home port of Donaghadee in Ireland to stock up and prepare for the voyage across the Atlantic. The contents of the hold would bring a tidy profit to MacDonald and MacLeod, and of course all the sailors were on a cut of the profits too, thus ensuring their complicity and silence.

Now all this clearly seemed a good deal to the lairds of Dunvegan and Sleat, but for the captives themselves the conditions were truly horrific. Cooped up below decks, most of them never having been out to sea further than for a stretch of inshore fishing, many were suffering from sea-sickness. For food they were given stale bread and buckets of water lowered from above. There were of course no toilet facilities as such, and the air quickly became foetid and oppressive as increasing numbers became ill. Two of the older women were so ill that it appeared they might die, and so the ship anchored briefly off the coast of Jura in order to send them ashore along with another woman who was in the final stages of pregnancy. This would appear to have been more a matter of expediency than any compassion on the part of Davidson. He had no wish to be troubled by any of the problems presented by either death or birth.

Arriving at Donaghadee on the east coast of Northern Ireland the *William* dropped anchor and the human cargo was taken ashore and marched under armed guard to a couple of farm buildings on the outskirts of the town. Here they were locked up while the crew went about the business of fitting out the ship and replenishing the stores ready for the voyage across the Atlantic. Davidson had ensured that the prisoners were in an out-of-the-way place so that no one would hear their piteous cries for help. It is easy to imagine the horror and discomfiture they were feeling. Only a couple of days previously they had been going about their lives as normal, and now here they were in a strange land, ready to be sent off to a life of slavery in countries they had only vaguely heard of. However, they were island people who were used to adversity and hardship, and when their cries for help remained unanswered it became clear that their only hope, if hope there was, was to stage an escape.

So the fittest of them proceeded to break their way out of the barns in which they were trapped. Working together, as they had always done, it wasn't too difficult to break through the walls and let themselves out. When the crew of the *William* returned they found most of their captives had fled. There were only eighteen of them left, mainly women with very young children, and some older folk. Word was sent back to Captain Davidson on the

William and his first action was to go to the local magistrate. Here he demanded that the militia be called out to help recapture the nearly ninety felons who had escaped. Furious at the possible disappearance of a big bonus for their transportation, his anger at the escapees was clear. The judge, however, was a diligent and honest man. When it came to matters of the law he was a stickler for detail and no jumped-up ship's captain would tell him how to go about his business.

His first action was to ask Davidson for a copy of the ship's manifest, the legal details of the ship's cargo, destination and other details. After looking over it in his office he spoke to Davidson: 'We seem to have a problem here, Captain Davidson. I see only six felons' names on the manifest, yet you appear to have over a hundred prisoners.'

'These criminals were given into my custody by gentlemen of standing in Scotland; in fact the chiefs of the clans these wretches were part of before they transgressed,' Davison replied.

'This is as may be, but I would be remiss in giving you a warrant to arrest these people without some further enquiry,' said the judge, fixing Davidson with a piercing stare. He was already sure something was amiss here. To have only six of these people on the manifest was strange indeed. In fact later he found out that though these six were guilty of crimes, they were extremely petty and certainly carried no threat of either imprisonment or transportation.

The judge wanted to find out just what was going on, and it didn't take long. By now the story of what had happened to these poor Scots was common knowledge in the area. As they had spread out into the countryside looking for food and shelter they had told their pitiful tale to all they met. Soon farmers and cottars who had heard the tale were streaming into Donaghadee, some of them bringing the Scots along with them. The judge immediately ordered that all of the Scots people who had escaped should come to the Court House and tell him their stories. One after another the same story was told, of how they had been lured on board the ship and imprisoned. How none of them, apart from the six petty offenders, had ever been charged with any crime and how in effect they had all been kidnapped.

Hearing these sad stories the judge was moved to comment. 'Never have I heard of such evil, and you poor people from Scotland are about the most miserable objects of compassion ever to come before me.'

Turning to the Clerk of the Court he then said. 'Issue immediate warrants for the arrests of Captain Davidson of the ship *William* and for Norman MacLeod from Harris in Scotland.'

This was done, and soldiers were sent to the ship to arrest the culprits, but by now, realising that the game as up they had made themselves scarce. Word of what had happened soon spread to Scotland, especially as some of the Harris people began making their way back home at once. Soon the scandal was common knowledge, and an official government inquiry was set up to find out what had happened. At a preliminary meeting of the inquiry it was noted that both MacDonald and MacLeod had shown a cynical regard for the bonds and obligation of kinship. This was a Lowland judge speaking and even he could see the depths of the venality and greed of these so-called Highland chiefs. At that point one of the most powerful men in Scotland stepped into the picture. This was Duncan Forbes of Culloden, a man close to government and one of the strongest Unionists in a Scotland that was awash with Jacobitism. He simply decreed that no inquiry should take place, and the matter was dropped. Public opinion however, noted the comments of the judge, even if justice was so blatantly denied. Neither of the lairds were ever punished for this monstrous kidnapping, but their lives were undoubtedly affected by what had happened.

This pair of greedy criminals had been involved in an earlier scandal. They had conspired with Lord Grange to kidnap and hide his wife Lady Grange after she had heard her husband plotting the return of Prince Charles Edward Stewart with Simon Fraser of Lovat and others. Lovat called on his friends MacDonald and MacLeod for help, and Lady Grange was whisked off to live out a pathetic existence as a prisoner on a series of isolated crofts in the Hebrides. Back in Edinburgh Grange claimed she was ill with a fever and then announced her death. He then staged a well-attended funeral. Despite this, rumours continued to circulate that the poor woman was still alive somewhere. The plotters then had her taken to the isolated island of St Kilda, the poorest and most old-fashioned society in Scotland. It was also a society where everyone spoke Gaelic, a language of which Lady Grange did not know a single word. After many years there she was returned to Skye, where matters improved slightly for her. She learned to spin and sent off a letter in a hank of wool going to Inverness. As she had no ink or pencil the letter was in fact written in her own blood.

Despite Grange's best efforts a ship sailed out to the Hebrides to try to locate her, and the poor woman was imprisoned in a cave on the shore of Loch Bracadale. From there she was again taken to the Isle of Uist, the boatman who took her having strict instructions to throw her overboard if a ship approached! She ended her days, still a prisoner, at Waternish in Skye just before Prince Charlie returned to start the '45.

Now Forbes of Culloden heard of what had happened in England and realised that this and the incident of the *William* would give him leverage over both MacDonald and MacLeod. The details may never be known, but it is clear that a deal was struck whereby MacDonald and MacLeod escaped prosecution on one condition – they were not to bring out their clans in support of the Stewarts! In fact, in the case of MacLeod he actually took his clansmen to reinforce Lord Loudon's regiment at Inverness in 1746, while some of his clansmen thought they were heading off to join Prince Charlie!

As for the prisoners from the *William*, some of them remained in Donaghadee, glad to be away from the hardships they had suffered at the hands of their own chiefs. A considerable number eventually returned to their own homes in the Hebrides, and we can imagine how they saw their clan chiefs from then onwards.

An Expensive Meal

Around the beginning of the seventeenth century a couple of MacGregors were returning from Glasgow towards their home on the Braes of Balquhidder. They were passing through the Lennox, the lands lying to the east of Loch Lomond. This was an area dominated by the Colquhouns with whom the Mac-Gregors had long been at feud. So, despite the laws of Highland hospitality, they were turned away from every clachan and house they approached to ask for food and shelter. After a few such refusals they began to feel resentful at this treatment. They discussed what to do. Well, they were hungry and they were MacGregors after all, so if they were not freely given hospitality they would just as freely take it. They decided that they fancied a bit of mutton, and therefore they would just help themselves to a sheep. After all, the Colquhouns around there had plenty sheep and would hardly miss one. They grabbed a fine-looking sheep and headed into the hills to find themselves a sheltered spot. Coming across an old bothy, or hut, they duly butchered the animal and began to prepare a meal. Now from all the beasts to hand they had chosen a particularly obvious animal, a black wedder, a castrated male sheep, with a white tail. Whether they had done this out of stupidity or bravado is impossible to tell, but within an hour someone noticed that the sheep had gone miss-ing. Suspicion immediately fell on the two passing MacGregors and the hunt was up. The Colquhouns needed little excuse to go after their hereditary enemies! Colquhoun of Luss was informed of the incident and he gathered together a group of men to look for the MacGregors. The two hungry travellers were discovered while they were still partaking of the meal which the missing beast had provided. There was no hesitation, and the two MacGregors were killed on the spot for their thievery.

Word of what had happened didn't take long to spread, and the relatives of the two travellers in Glen Gyle and Glen Strae and around Loch Katrine soon knew what had happened to their missing men. The ancient enmity against the Colquhouns needed little stoking at the best of times to burst into action, but this killing in cold blood was a blatant provocation. Patrick MacGregor of Laggarie came down with a raiding party upon Glen Fruin and lifted a fair number of cattle from a farm near Strone. In doing this he ignored the right of 'gyrth', or 'garth', a form of sanctuary extending three miles around Luss kirk that had been granted by Robert the Bruce. In such areas people could claim sanctuary from all law and to raid in such an area was extremely provocative. By breaking these ancient customs the MacGregors were heaping up troubles for themselves in the years ahead. And this was just the start.

In July 1592, the MacGregors came again, this time with some men of the Macfarlane clan. They came down from the north through Glen Fruin and lifted all the cattle and other beasts they could find in the lands west of Loch Lomond. They seemed to be making a particular point of ravaging the possessions of the Colquhouns. Humphrey Colquhoun of Bannachra gathered together a force of his own and attacked the raiders. After a bloody fight Humphrey and the remainder of the Colquhoun forces were forced to retreat and take shelter in Bannachra Castle, to the east of the modern town of Helensburgh.

The raiders from the north then laid siege to the castle. Now Bannachra Castle was a substantial building, well stocked with provisions, so no doubt Humphrey thought he could simply sit out the siege and wait for the cateran forces to become fed-up and leave. They however had other plans. Somehow they were in touch with one of the Colquhouns in the castle. For whatever reason – money, or a dislike of Humphrey – he agreed to help the besiegers. One evening, not long after the siege had begun, he was accompanying Humphrey up the spiral staircase in the tower of the castle. He was just behind, and was carrying a torch, the light of which clearly outlined Humphrey just as they passed one of the windows on the tower. At once there was a whooshing sound. Straight through the narrow window came an arrow which pierced Humphrey through the heart! This took the fight out of the local resistance and the MacGregors and the Macfarlanes were able to advance north via Glen Fruin with their spoils, without having to bother about pursuit.

Now inter-clan raiding had been part of Scottish society since the Iron Age, and Lowland areas abutting the Highlands were always being raided. It was an integral part of the life of the clan warriors, and though Lowland society might see it as theft, the Highlanders considered such raiding to be a suitable activity for Highland gentlemen, which effectively meant it was suitable for every man. The raiding on the Colquhouns though had become little more than a blood-feud. It would seem that the MacGregors were of the opinion that the price of the black wedder with the white tail was still not fully paid.

In early December 1602 Duncan MacEwan MacGregor of Glen Strae came to the Colquhoun lands again with a party of eighty men. They came down on Glen Finlas, as usual gathering all the cattle they could find and driving off. Cattle were still the main form of moveable wealth among the Highland clans, and for many of the Lowland areas too. This was a successful raid, in that Duncan and his associates acquired more than 300 cattle, with even more sheep, goats and horses. They headed back to the north to divide up their spoil, with the intention of trading some of the stock to other clans. Colquhoun of Rossdhu, the castle overlooking the waters of Loch Lomond just north of Glen Finglas, was unable to stop this large force making off with their booty. However, if he could not beat them in battle he resolved to have his revenge another way.

Aware that the king, James VI, was currently at Stirling he devised a strategy to bring royal power to bear against the MacGregors. He gathered together a large group of local women and told them what they had to do. So it was that a day later a sombre convoy of mounted women arrived to see the king at the ancient royal seat of Stirling. Each of these women claimed to be the widow of a goodman killed in battle with the thieving Highlanders, and to emphasise the point Humphrey had provided each with a 'bludie sark' or shirt held high on a spear. In truth the shirts had all been dipped in the blood of a few sheep slaughtered for the purpose. The cynical pageant rode into the town, all of the women wailing and keening over their supposed loss. This had the desired effect. The king was outraged at the sight of these poor women and had no hesitation in granting Colquhoun's request. This was to issue Letters of Fire and Sword, legal documents which effectively allowed the pursuit and slaughter of those named in the letters. This was more than just being declared outlaw; this was an excuse for what could be seen as something close to genocide. Over the centuries such letters were often given out by Scottish kings, in many cases being given to one clan to hound another. The old adage of 'set a thief to catch a thief' was something to which the Scottish kings were happy to ascribe, plagued as they constantly were by the fact that the royal writ was so often ignored by the warriors of the Highland clans and their chiefs.

But the MacGregors were fierce warriors themselves and Alisdair of Glen Strae had no intention of waiting for his lands to be invaded and his people slaughtered. He would take the initiative against his enemies.

With a force of 300 men Alisdair marched down through Glen Fruin to strike at the Colquhouns. With him were many experienced warriors, including the famous Iain Dubh nan Lurach, Black John of the Corselet, so known for the fact that he never, ever took off his body-armour except to wash, and that was probably not too often! Along with them came a contingent of their hereditary allies, the MacFarlanes, one of the Highland clans most addicted to cattle-raiding. In fact they were so notorious that in the south-west of Scotland the harvest moon was known as MacFarlane's Lantern, as it was in the long moonlit nights of autumn that the raiders loved best to ply their trade. There was also a good sprinkling of other clans: Mac-Donalds and Macleans of Glencoe; Robertsons, Macleans and some from that other great raiding clan the Camerons. Records tell that they carried a range of weapons: halberds, poleaxes, the ubiquitous two-handed swords, bows and arrows and hagbuts, early muskets and pistols. While some of these weapons would be carried on a normal raid, this was something more. The MacGregors understood they were effectively at war with the King's representatives.

Alexander Colquhoun knew of their coming and had gathered a considerable force of his own. He had called in allies from all over the Lennox as well as a group of burgesses from Dumbarton. They moved up Glen Fruin with a force of over 300 on foot and another 500 on horseback. Now Colquhoun expected Alisdair's force to come down in one large group and intended ambushing them in Glen Fruin. Accordingly, he divided his force into two, half of whom were supposed to let the Mac-Gregors pass and then fall on them from behind. They would catch the raiders between the two groups and destroy them. Well, that's what Alexander planned. However, in the heavily wooded slopes of Glen Fruin there was no advantage in having mounted warriors. Also on the day Alisdair, a wily and experienced warrior, had split his force in two as well.

So on that fateful day of 7 February, 1603, the Battle of Glen Fruin took place. The MacGregor contingents were at the head of the Glen while their companions were in hiding near the farm of Strone. The Colquhouns came into the glen from Luss through Glen Mackurn. As they pushed on, hoping to find the MacGregors beyond the narrow pass and allow time for their own ambush to be set, they came up against Alisdair, whose troops were settled in the glen itself. Meanwhile the other Gregorach, under Alisdair's brother John, came round behind their enemies. The Colquhouns found themselves caught between two forces of Gregorach. Alexander's plan had worked, but for his enemies.

Caught between two forces, the mounted contingent became a liability as the horses were forced into one another. There was no way they could find a space to rally and charge. They were driven into boggy ground at Achingaich, where their problems worsened in the boggy ground. To escape they would have to fight their way through the enemy lines. The Colquhouns had called for vengeance and the MacGregors knew it. There was to be no mercy that day. To fall into the hands of the MacGregors meant instant death, and over 140 Colquhouns alone are said to have died. Buchanan of Buchlyvie fought well and killed several MacGregors before he was cut down, and many of the locals put up a good fight. Iain Dubh nan Larach fell in the heat of the battle and was buried nearby.

Then something occurred which has long blotted the honour of the MacGregors. A party of scholars from the Collegiate College at Dumbarton had come out early in the day to sit above Glen Fruin to watch the battle. They had been assured by Alexander and his friends that they would see a great victory over the wild men from the north! In the heat of the battle though it seems that these young men were mistaken for potential fighting men and were slaughtered by the Gregorach. Well, that is what the Gregorach will say, though their enemies said it was nothing more nor less than cold-blooded massacre of the innocents. After the procession of 'bludie sarks' at Stirling the matter is perhaps still debatable. Whatever caused it, it was yet another action that was used to justify the widespread and brutal suppression of Clan Gregor.

Once the Colquhoun force was scattered and destroyed the Gregorach could concentrate on the rest of their business. Hundreds of cattle and sheep were rounded up and driven off, and farm after farm was burned to the ground. In fact they 'lifted' so many cattle that the victorious MacGregors had trouble herding them all, and sold many of them to other clans on their journey homewards to Glenstrae.

Alexander Colquhoun's plan had come to nothing, and he had merely made matters worse for his own kin. He managed to escape the slaughter of the battle and holed up in Bunnachra Castle. However, he wasn't the only one who had an agenda. Watching over matters was MacCalien Mor, the head of Glen Campbell and Earl of Argyll. When the king heard of the disastrous battle of Glen Fruin it seems that he listened to some advice from MacCailien Mor. Without troubling to find out what the MacGregors might have to say in their own defence, an act was passed in the Privy Council on 3 April, 1603. This was only days before James VI left Scotland for England to take possession of the English throne and to concern himself for the rest of his life with 'bigger things'! The Act effectively gave Campbell carte-blanche in dealing with the MacGregors, whose lands adjoining his own he had for so long coveted.

Under the provisions of the act the very name of Gregor or MacGregor was forever abolished. All those who bore the name were commanded, under penalty of death, to change it for another; giving the traditional hospitality of the Highlands to any person named MacGregor was also to be punished, by death. This ran against hundreds of years of tradition, but MacCailien Mor was intent on destroying the power of the MacGregors forever. The Act also declared that any men on the MacGregor side at the Battle of Glen Fruin, or who took part in the subsequent despoliation of the lands of Luss, was henceforward prohibited, again under penalty of death, from carrying weapons of any kind other than a pointless knife to eat their meat. This was clearly ridiculous in a society where every man went about armed. If the MacGregors obeyed this law they would be incapable of defending themselves at a time when much of the country was actively persecuting them; if they didn't they were condemned anyway! Some of these conditions were not actually repealed until 1775!

The hunt was on and being prosecuted with extraordinary venom. Around eighty of the participants in the battle were named and a bounty was put on their heads, making them the target of anyone who thought they could kill or capture them, anywhere, anytime. Warrants for the killing of the Gregorach were then put up throughout Scotland, effectively designating them as animals who it was legal for anyone to hunt! Bloodhounds, *conn dubh* in Gaelic – black dogs – were used to track the Gregorach, and stories have survived that some of these dogs were bred with a diet of nothing but MacGregor flesh to make them even better at hunting their prey. The king had long wanted to pacify the Highland clans and was happy to let MacCailein Mor do as he saw fit with the MacGregors.

So the long-term persecution of the Children of the Mist began. Acts against them were passed in 1611, 1613, 1621 and 1627. These last two were to continue the proscriptions against the rising generation of MacGregors, and in 1633 the king, Charles I, down in London, issued fresh Letters of Fire and Sword, this time going so far as to prohibit priests from baptising or christening the children of the MacGregors! This was at a time when it was generally believed that, if a baby died un-christened, it would not be entitled to enter heaven. Nothing it seems was too horrible to be visited on the Gregorach. Many of the clan fought on and lived like guerrillas, while yet others adopted other names and attempted to live normal lives. It is one of the ironies of history that so many of them, including that debatable character, Rob Roy MacGregor, actually chose the name Campbell! What cannot be doubted is that the meal made from the black wedder with the white tail proved a very expensive one for the MacGregor clan!

A Cruel and Savage Chief

The nature of clan society was such that while the chiefs never had absolute feudal control over their clansmen some of them were undoubtedly despotic. One such was Donald MacDonald of Castle Tioram, which sits high on a rocky tidal island in Loch Moidart to the north of the Ardnamurchan Peninsula. He had been heavily involved on the Royalist side in the campaigns of Montrose in the middle of the seventeenth century. As ever, when war and religion are mixed, there was a great deal of brutality in the struggle between Parliament and the Stewart dynasty, and it may be that the bloodletting of the period coarsened Donald's character. Be that as it may, he was known to be prone to sentencing even those guilty of minor crimes to death, under the powers of the Baron Baillie court in which he sat as judge. He was also effectively the jury and the executioner. Not that he was alone in that at this period. In fact for a couple of hundred years or more the British government was happy to see poor people hanged for thefts which nowadays would be at most the cause of a fine or community service.

On one occasion Donald was robbed of a considerable sum of money, but was unable to prove that the suspects, his valet, a friend of his and a local lass, known simply as James's daughter, had committed the crime. There was no evidence against them. This however mattered little to Donald, and he had the two men hanged, but subjected the poor lass to an even worse fate. Her hands and feet were bound and she was taken out to a rock a couple of hundred yards off Castle Tioram. Here she was tied by her hair to the seaweed and left for the rising tide to drown her.

The rock was ever after known as *Sgeir nighinn-t-Sheumais* [the rock of James's daughter], the poor lass not even being named. On another occasion Donald hanged his cook who, addicted to snuff, had had the temerity to take Donald's own snuff-mill! The story is that, although guilty as charged, she somehow managed to secrete the snuff-mill about her person, and taking a last pinch before being hanged outside the walls of Castle Tioram, she threw the mill into the sea.

Now Donald, like most Highlanders, was extremely fond of hunting and he had a favourite gun that he called *A Chubag* [the Cuckoo]. As he got older and less able to chase deer through the hills he liked nothing better than to sit on the battlements of Castle Tioram and take pot-shots at whatever took his fancy. This soon led to the extermination of most animals and birds in the immediate vicinity the castle, but one day he was looking out from his favourite spot for something to shoot at when he saw what he thought was a suspicious character on a rock opposite the castle. The man was close to a small group of sheep browsing nearby, and Donald immediately jumped to the conclusion that here was a thief getting ready to steal some of his sheep! With advancing years Donald's eyesight was not quite what it had been, and he did not recognise the man at all. However, he could see clearly enough that this man was lurking near some of his sheep! He brought 'the Cuckoo' to bear on the figure and fired off a shot. His eyesight was still good enough to take good aim. The man was bowled over and fell off the rock. At once some of the people in the castle went running over to the spot, where they found one of the finest young men of the clan lying there dead, with his head in a spring that sprouted from the foot of the rock he had been sitting on. He had been at a bit of a loose end and had simply been lying on the rock, enjoying the warmth of the sun.

As for Donald, he showed no remorse; he had thought him a thief and it was simply the young lad's own fault for having put himself in such danger. The servants in the castle were by this time so cowed by the brutality of their master that none raised a murmur. The young man's fall had landed him head first in the well and from then on it was referred to as *Tobar-nan-ceann* [the well of the head].

In his general thuggishness Donald was no respecter of persons, age, or anything else at all. On one occasion he was amongst the MacDonalds out on the island of Uist when he came across a party of his clanspeople taking a break from cutting peats. This was a communal task when all the members of a community would go together to cut and stack peats, allowing them to dry out and provide fuel for their fires through out the winter. The fires were used both for heating and cooking and the cutting of the peat was a central activity of many Highland and Island communities since time immemorial. In some areas it continues to this day. Now on this particular day the people cutting the peat had brought a side of mutton with them, and when the meal was finished an old man, reputed to be a bit of a prophet, raised the shoulder-blade of the sheep and squinted at it. This was one of the traditional means of divining the future that long lingered among the ostensibly Christian people of the Western Isles. The gift of the Second Sight was well known, and those blessed, or perhaps cursed, with such an ability, were generally well respected amongst their communities, and perhaps a little feared.

'What do you see there?' growled Donald in his usual surly fashion.

'Ach well,' replied the old man. 'I am afraid I see something that Clanranald would not like to be knowing.'

'Tell me, now, at once,' demanded the clan chief.

'If you say so,' said the old man slowly, 'but I can see that the Clanranald lands will be broken up into many small pieces in time to come.'

Incensed by this vision of the future the chief whipped out his dirk and stabbed the old man through the heart!

It was not long afterwards that Donald went after someone even more respected within the community. For some unknown reason Donald had imprisoned a woman of the clan in a small castle on the island of Canna. The priest on the island brought this up in his Sunday sermon. In fact he went farther and proceeded to describe the chief of the MacDonalds in extremely unflattering terms, making it clear that he found his actions unacceptable. On hearing of this, Donald's by now famous temper exploded. Who did this upstart priest think he was, criticising him? He wasted no time, and set sail for Canna, with his trusty 'Cuckoo' by his side. The priest's profession was no defence against the chief's anger and lust for revenge. How dare this jumped-up black crow of a priest dare to criticise him! Luckily the priest saw the chief's galley coming to the island and managed to run off and hide in the western part of Canna. Donald hunted the entire island for the priest, and the longer the hunt continued the more it became apparent what the intended outcome was to be . . . Donald clearly meant to send the interfering priest to meet his maker. The island people however knew well that he was out of order, and after a fruitless day of searching, a group of them went to the priest and took him to a boat which transported him to Skye. This was outside Donald's lands and the priest would be safe there.

From then on things got worse, if not for the clan, then certainly for Donald himself. It began to be noticed that wherever Donald went he was followed by a huge black toad. No one knows how, but it just turned up and made its home at Castle Tioram, and no one had any doubt that it was a supernatural and probably a diabolical creature. Donald was never seen to try and kill it, and it made a habit of following him wherever he went. Once he sneaked out of the castle into his birlinn, and sailed away to Loch Boisdale before the sun was up, leaving the toad sleeping by the fire in the hall. On arriving at Loch Bosidale who should await him but the toad. On another similar occasion, having left the toad behind, he was angry when he realised it was swimming along behind his boat. The longer the black creature hung around, the darker grew Donald's moods, and he kept trying to escape to one or other of the Hebridean islands. Increasingly, as he did so the toad seemed to call up wild and dangerous weather and it began to openly appear resentful of these attempts. On one such occasion the weather grew gradually worse till the chief's birlinn was in the heart of a vicious storm with the toad swimming in circles around the boat, which was heaving and tossing to such an extent that the oarsmen began to call on their chief to let the thing on board before it sank them all! Donald fiercely ignored these requests, even taking the tiller of the boat himself to try and steer a course for dry land. And all the time the creature swam around the boat, keeping its eye on him. At last when it seemed as if the boat could not survive he called to the toad to come aboard. As soon as it did so the storm subsided.

No one had any doubt that this evil-looking creature was connected with the Devil and it was generally thought that Donald was probably caught up in some dreadful Satanic contract with Auld Hornie himself. On the night he died Donald was lying in his bed, with no sign of the obnoxious black creature that had dogged his steps for so many years, when a loud whistling was heard. Perhaps it was the toad – perhaps it was something – else but whatever it was it had an immediate effect. The dying man clapped his hands over his ears and tried to rise from his bed, but didn't have the strength. The whistling continued, and a look of horror came over the old man's face. Again he struggled to arise from his bed, his hands still clasped over his ears and a look of utter terror in his eyes. As the whistling got even louder he managed to stagger from his bed, bumping into the furniture around the room, moaning dreadfully, tears flowing from his staring eyes and his hands still locked to his ears. He was then tied to his bed and spent the rest of night writhing and moaning as the whistling continued. At last as the sun rose a sound came over the eerie whistling. It was the sound of a cock crowing, and as the sun rose into the sky Donald MacDonald passed away. None there that day had any doubt that he had gone to meet the master of the black toad that had haunted his steps for so many years.

Magic and Superstition

⪢◆⪡

The MacLeods and the Fairies

Belief in the fairies was strong amongst the Highland clans, and went hand in hand with their Christian beliefs. It is as if people thought that when Christianity first came to the Highlands it was a fine new religion but that certain aspects of the old ways of thinking about the world retained some of their usefulness, and so were carried on. This led to the situation where such pagan customs as animal sacrifices to try and stop cattle disease were still practised even as late as the eighteenth century in some districts. The belief in the fairies lasted even longer, and there are many tales of pipers being lured away to fairy residences inside notable hills or underground. It wasn't only musicians that the fairies were after though.

Far back in the thirteenth century, the third chief of the MacLeods, Malcolm, married the daughter of the Earl of Mar and soon afterwards she gave birth to a healthy, bonny laddie that they called Iain. It was always a grand thing when a chief's heir was born and the clanspeople celebrated his birth with some vigour. As he began to grow it was obvious that he was both strong and fit and of a happy nature, and the whole clan were proud of their chief's new boy. One day in Dunvegan Castle however, a dreadful scene occurred. Iain had been left sleeping by his mother behind a curtain in an alcove off the main room at Dunvegan. After a while she drew back the curtain to check on her baby who had been sleeping quietly for a while. There was no one there. She screamed, and at once everyone in the fort came running. There was no sign of the child and no one had been seen near to where he had been left sleeping. No one had any idea of what had happened. Had the boy been kidnapped by some other clan? Had one of their own people taken him? At once a search of the immediate area around Dunvegan was organised. Every one in the area was questioned, but no one had seen anything. It was as if the boy had simply disappeared into thin air. Suspicion fell on the MacDonalds, but they had had nothing whatsoever to do with the child's disappearance. A great sadness fell on the MacLeods. Their future chief had simply vanished and no one had any idea at all of what had happened. His poor mother was almost insane with grief, and the MacLeod himself was driving himself mad trying to conjecture what might have happened. Some of the older women in particular were sure they knew what had happened. The fairies must have got him. Now if humans had taken Iain something could have been done they said, but up against the supernatural powers of the little people there was nothing that could be done. However, life must go on, and soon things were getting back to normal amongst the MacLeods. Almost. The MacLeod and his lady were stricken with sadness, and Dunvegan was not a happy place.

The autumn and winter passed, and the following spring the lassies and lads went off to the shielings. Among them was Morag MacCrimmon, daughter of the hereditary piper to the MacLeods. One day, going back to the simple shieling huts the young people occupied in the high pastures during the summer months, she ripped her dress on a sharp rock, close by the tumbled ruins of an ancient fortress or dun. Like the rest of the women she always carried a needle and thread with her and she sat on a rock to mend the tear. Sitting there sewing she gradually became aware of a gentle humming coming from somewhere nearby. Being the daughter of a piper, and a Mac-Crimmon at that, she had been raised in a house full of music.

She had developed a good ear, and soon realised that the sound was that of a song. It seemed to be coming directly from the ground beneath her feet. Being a clever lass she stopped her sewing and stuck her needle into the ground, putting the end of the tightly stretched thread to her ear. With the sound thus amplified she began to make out the words of a song; it was a lullaby, and it told of the capture of a baby boy and his subsequent stay amongst the little people, the fairies. This could only be about wee Iain, she thought. As soon as she realised this she headed for Dunvegan, where she ran to find the chief's wife and told her what she had heard. At once the chief was sent for. He came back from another part of the island where he had been visiting and was told about what had happened. It made sense. No one had seen anything that day Iain had disappeared. Those who had said that the fairies must have taken him were right. MacLeod sent messengers to all the clachans of the MacLeods to ask anyone with knowledge of the People of Peace to come to see him right away. Soon a few people came in: a couple of old women reputed to have the second sight and another who had herself been stolen away by the fairies as a child before being rescued by her grandmother, a wise woman, some would even say a witch. But witches work with the white powers well as the black, and most Highland people were well aware that there were some among them who still possessed the knowledge of the olden times. So they all met together with MacLeod and his wife, and it was agreed that the fairies had most likely hidden Iain away within the walls of the old dun. After a long discussion it was decided that the best plan for rescuing wee Iain was to wait for *Samhain* [Sow-een], which we now call Halloween. That was the night when the boundaries between the worlds were at their thinnest and some of the ancestral dead, as well as creatures of the supernatural world, walked among the living. At that point the power of the fairies would be strong, but human intervention into their world would be possible.

Getting a changeling or a kidnapped child back from under the power of the Little People was always going to be difficult, but *Samhain* would provide the best chance. On that most eerie of all nights it was weel-kennt that the fairies would stream out from their underground houses to dance as long as the moon was up. The night of *Samhain* came, and a party of experienced warriors, led by their chief, accompanied by MacCrimmon the piper and his daughter, went back up to the shieling. Waiting nearby till the moon came up and the fairies left their hiding-place the men moved slowly and quietly into the ragged walls of the old fortress. A light was spotted through a chink in a tumbledown wall. Looking through the old stones they saw a child in a cradle with an old woman sitting beside him. Surely this must be the chief's son! The woman beside his cradle appeared to be human, and there was no sign of any of the fairies. Slowly and carefully moving the old stones the men cleared a space to climb through. The first one through was MacLeod himself, and the old woman turned to look at him as he half-fell through the gap. As the hood fell from her head he saw that this was certainly no fairy – it was old Margaret from Colbost. She had disappeared one day not long after Iain had gone. She had been out collecting shellfish on the shore when a sudden storm came up. It had been assumed she had been swept out to sea. Now it was clear that she had been kidnapped to look after the human child.

'Och it's yourself, MacLeod,' she said, bursting into tears, 'the wee lad is here and he is well. Oh praise the Lord you have come for us.'

MacLeod went to the cradle and looked in to see his son sleeping soundly.

'Ay, it is a fine thing we have found you Margaret. Let's be out of here quick'. He spoke as a couple of the other men came through the gap in the wall that was growing as their companions removed more stones. MacLeod reached down and picked up his son, a fierce light of gladness in his eye. Clutching the bairn to his chest, he turned to the men beside him.

'Give Margaret a hand and let's be out of here,' he commanded. So the baby was brought out from the ancient ruin and MacLeod, Morag and the clansmen headed back, a couple of the men helping Margaret, by now babbling with joy at her release, to get down the steep slopes. As they went back MacCrimmmon unshipped his pipes and began to play the fairy lullaby his daughter had been humming to him ever since she first heard it.

The sound of the pipes preceded them, and well before they reached Dunvegan Iain's mother met them on the road. By now the wee lad was wide awake and by the time they reached the fort itself most of the clan had gathered to welcome him home. There was great rejoicing in Dunvegan Castle that night, and for many days after, and from that time onwards the fairy lullaby was always the tune used to lull the MacLeod bairns to sleep.

The Magic Candle

As late as the nineteenth century *corp creaghs* were still being used in Scotland. These were clay images of people that were used to try and work ill against individuals, and closely resembled the similar magic tool, the wax image. This black magic type of practice has been known in many societies and the custom was generally to stick pins in the image in order to cause pain and even death in the intended victim. One old clan tale involves not a wax image but something that was claimed to be just as powerful – a wax candle!

Back in the early years of the eighteenth century at Beinn nan Gall in Strathnairn, Farquhar McGillivray, sixth chieftain of Dunmaglas, had a son called William. Now William grew up to be a fine, fit, healthy lad but he also happened to be rather good-looking. When he grew up he took over the position of Clan

Captain, by now a refined variation on the war-band leaders of earlier times, but still requiring the office-holder to be a capable fighter and a good strategist. William was given the name '*Caiptin Ban*' – the Fair Captain. Generally this would have meant 'fair-coloured', but there seems little doubt that William was a handsome man, and one it seems with a strong interest in the fairer sex.

Now one of his neighbours, a man of some standing himself, had taken a wife, Amelie, who was considered something of a beauty. It is just a fact of nature that some men cannot refrain from treating their spouses almost as if they were trophies, particularly older men, and it is likely that the gentleman concerned was a good deal older than his wife. Whatever the case, there can be no doubt that he was deeply in love with his young wife. You can imagine his horror then, when one day she simply disappeared. No one had seen her leave their house, she had not been seen by anyone on the district and despite search parties scouring the area there was absolutely no sign of the bonnie young lass.

At first the distraught husband hoped that whatever had happened would prove to be a passing thing, and that she would soon turn up. Sadly, however, the weeks began to pass with no sight or sign of her at all. Now although Christianity had long been the official religion in Scotland the belief in fairies and other forms of magic had not disappeared, and there were those who muttered that she must have been spirited away by the fairies. It was said that she had been spirited away inside the fairy mound of Tomnashangan. The husband dismissed such ideas as no more than rank superstition; he was a rational, modern Christian gentleman and would have no truck with such notions. Still the rumours circulated, though not all believed the fairies had anything to do with the situation, and as the weeks passed he became ever more desperate. At last, at the suggestion of a friend, who perhaps knew more than he was letting on, the husband was induced to go and ask for help from William MacGillivary, the Fair Captain.

So he headed off to speak to William at Beinn Nan Gall, where his family had lived for generations. William sat in his living room and listened attentively to the man's problems. He looked thoughtful, and after pacing up and down the room for a while he spoke.

'Well, I know a few people who have what we might call some of the old knowledge – I do not want to say too much about that,' he said, 'but I will ask around and see if anything can be found out. Leave it with me for a few days and I will be in touch.'

He then showed his visitor out.

A week later William arrived at the man's door with some truly odd information.

'I have asked around the oldest and wisest people of the district,' he said, 'and they are all agreed that your wife has been spirited away by the fairies.'

'That is preposterous. Nothing but superstition,' blustered the husband. 'I have never heard such nonsense in all my life. How can an educated man like yourself believe this rubbish?'

It was clear that the man would take some convincing, but William told him there was a way of maybe getting his wife back, if only he would let him try.

'There is a man called MacQueen,' William declared, 'who has specific candles that have power over the fairies and I think I can lay my hands on one of them.'

'Well, even so, what good would that do?' came the reply.

'Well,' said William, with an odd look, 'Some of my acquaintances know how such things can be used and if you will allow me I will get their help and see if we can fetch your wife back.'

'Well, I still think it is a load of superstitious tripe,' said the husband, 'but if you want to try it I suppose you should go ahead. I just don't accept that fairies can have anything to do with this.'

'With your permission then,' said the Captain, 'I will go and try to reclaim your wife.'

Now the husband was in a depressed state and had just about come to the conclusion that his wife was dead. Perhaps she had fallen into the river and been washed out to sea, or something equally horrible had happened, and she had been murdered and buried in some out-of-the-way spot. He could not help himself thinking these horrible thoughts but he also could not stop hoping that she was still alive and would return to him some day. He was confused and deeply saddened and although he thought he was clutching at straws he wondered if perhaps MacGillivary could do something.

MacGillivary sent a messenger to John Dubh MacQueen of Pollochaik asking him for one of his candles. Now John was believed to have long been a familiar of the fairies and was held in awe by many of his neighbours. When the Captain's messenger came and delivered his message, John agreed to let him have one of the magic candles – at a price – but gave him very specific instructions.

'Now,' he said, 'on the way back to Dunmaglass you must never look behind you. You might hear a noise like a horse and carriage coming fast upon you and a voice shouting "Catch him, catch him", but whatever you do, do not turn round. If you do the least that can happen to you is that you will lose the candle; but it might be something much worse. Do you understand?'

'Aye, I won't look round no matter what I hear,' said the clearly nervous messenger.

So he set off, hearing his heart-beat sound in his ears and feeling sweat break out on his skin. Night began to fall when he was just at Craiganuin, near Moy Hall, when he heard the sound of horses behind him. There was also eldritch music in the air and he clearly heard cries of 'Catch him, catch him'. By now he was so frightened that he could not stop himself from looking over his shoulder. He saw nothing, but just at that moment he fell from his horse and dropped the candle. Just then the noises stopped. Getting back to his feet he scrabbled around, but not a trace of his candle could be seen. He spent over an hour searching for it, but there was no sign of it at all.

When he got back to Dunmaglass William MacGillivary was furious with him. The next day he sent another man to Mac-Queen, this time giving him clear instructions to do exactly as he was told. This messenger was made of sterner stuff and ignored the noises he heard which began just at the same place. However, further up the road at Farr the noises got louder and louder, until they were ten times as loud as they had been at first, and despite himself he too looked in fear over his shoulder. Again nothing was to be seen, but again he fell from his horse and yet again, the candle disappeared.

On hearing the news the Fair Captain realised that he was being tested and sent a third messenger the following day. This MacGillivary came through the first trial and the second, but when he came to the Findhorn river he found it in spate. There had been no heavy rainfall, so he realised that there was some-thing magical about this. But he was a man of strong character, and he simply rode all the way back to Pollochaik to ask MacQueen what to do. On receiving his instructions he rode back to the river, all the time ignoring the noises of galloping horses, the eldritch music and the shrill cries of 'Catch him, catch him'.

On reaching the river bank he dismounted and picked up a stone, just as he had been told. Taking a deep breath he threw the stone across the river. All at once he found himself mounted, on the other bank. Without waiting to think about matters at all he spurred his horse and headed off through the hills towards Dunmaglass. Although he could still hear the spooky noises around him he never flinched, and in the early hours of the morning he returned with the candle intact!

With the magic candle now in his possession William put the

next stage of his plan into action. On a moonlit night, just as the gloaming shaded into dark, he came up to Tomanshangan, the candle clasped firmly in his left hand. He had already spied out the mound on several occasions and knew where the entrance was. Sure enough, as the darkness began to fall he saw the outline of the door appear. Gently he put his hand on the door knob and turned it. The door swung inwards and he stepped into the pitch-black interior and heard the fairy music. Immediately the candle burst into light. There before him was Amelie dancing a reel, the rest of the company appearing as nothing more than shifting shadows. Taking her by the arm and protected by the power of the candle he pulled her out into the open air. There she told him she thought she had been dancing for only an hour or two instead of the months that had indeed passed.

You can imagine the delight of the husband when on the following day he was looking out of his window and saw William riding up with another horse following. And riding that horse was none other than the beautiful Amelie. He ran out to meet them, almost crying with joy. As his wife dismounted he clasped her his arms and burst into tears. The three of them then went into the house where William told him the story of what he had had to go through in order to rescue the fairy victim.

As for Amelie, she maintained she had no memory of anything at all, other than dancing for a few hours in the fairy hill. She did not know how she had even got there! It was all a complete mystery to her. She felt she had been dancing for an hour or so when William MacGillivary took her by the hand and led her from the fairy mound. She could tell her husband nothing more. A combination of relief at having his wife back and perhaps a touch of circumspection made him accept all that was said. He had no more questions. MacGillivary was thanked profusely and oaths of lifelong affection were sworn. William solemnly gave him the wax candle that had proved so efficacious in securing the return of his wife and it was kept in the family for several generations.

However, not long after this the Fair Captain was set upon by a bunch of ruffians one evening as he rode home along the shores of Loch Duntelchaig. He recognised none of them and they gave him a severe thrashing. His horse was so seriously injured in the attack that it had to be put down. And there were those in the area who doubted the power of the fairies, and said maybe Amelie's husband had figured it all out in the end!

A Change in the Weather

For many centuries the Lords of the Isles and their clansmen were virtually independent and probably few of them thought of themselves as even Scottish. Some of them were even prepared to ally with the English in their struggles with the Scottish king. While there may not be any ethnic difference between the peoples of the Highlands and Lowlands of Scotland, the language, culture and society of the Gaels made them a race apart. Brought up from birth with the notion that honour and battle were the warrior's way they regularly took the stance that their enemy's enemy was their friend. If this meant using the help of the English in their battles with the Scottish kings, what of it? They were all Southrons and foreigners anyway!

When his father Alisdair died in 1461, John, Lord of the Isles, entered into a treaty with Edward IV of England and with Earl Douglas who held extensive lands in the Scottish Borders. Like the Lords of the Isles the Douglases had long fought against the centralising policies of the Stewart kings in Edinburgh. Under a treaty signed at Ardtornish Castle overlooking the Sound of Mull in 1462, John, his cousin Donald Balloch, Earl of Ross, and the Douglas would become de facto rulers of their respective parts of Scotland in the event of the defeat of James II and the English conquest of Scotland. The long-term English policy of trying to assimilate Scotland into England would of course have made any such arrangement merely a temporary one, but both Donald and the Douglas failed to see this.

In 1476 this clandestine treaty came to light, and John was immediately declared a traitor by James III. Like many of the great clan chiefs he held several positions under the crown as part of the ongoing attempt to control and pacify the Highlands. James took away the Sherrifdoms of Inverness and Nairn as well as the Earldom of Ross from John. Now sometimes this type of action was little more than cosmetic – clan chiefs traditionally held their lands *a ghlaive* [by the sword] – and a declaration in Edinburgh without it being backed up by military action could sometimes simply be ignored. However, the Earl of Atholl was intent on capturing John. He sent out spies to discover where the fugitive was drawing his water; he then ordered that the well be filled with a mixture of whisky, honey and oatmeal, so as to beguile him into staying put while he surrounded the place. Thus was Lord John captured, and thus came into being 'Atholl Brose'.

All of this infuriated Angus Og, who seems to have been a man with a short fuse. He considered the king's actions to be an insult to his father, himself and all his clan and decided there was only one course of action to take. The Highland warriors had been addicted to raiding since at least Roman times, and probably even earlier, so what happened next was only to be expected. Angus gathered up a large force of MacDonalds and their allies and launched a major raid on Kintail, sweeping through the countryside and lifting all the cattle he could find. In those far-off days of the fifteenth century cattle were the main wealth of the clans and the chiefs counted their riches more by the number of cows and bulls they had than any gold or silver they might possess. Angus's force then swept north-east into Ross-shire and came up against the MacKenzies in a fierce battle at Lagabread.

Stories of this battle tell us that the ravens of Clan Donald enjoyed the fruits of the victory to the full. By now, most of the north of Scotland was aware that Angus Og was on the warpath, though it is unclear how much of this was caused by his supposed pique and how much by the opportunity for widespread raiding. The Earls of Huntly, Gordon and Crawford combined forces to stop Angus harrying their lands, but they too were defeated and a serious situation was developing. The Lords of the Isles were always a thorn in the side of the civil government of Scotland, and now it seemed as though Angus Og was intent on defeating all possible opposition.

Down in Argyll the Chief of Clan Campbell began to think that he would be the next to feel the thrust of the Clan Donald campaign. Like many of his clan he was an adept politician as well as a skilled warrior, and he thought long and hard about what he could do. Clearly, he thought, the first thing to do would be to get a royal edict from James to raise an army against Angus Og. This would allow him to recruit troops from may other clans and would substantially increase his forces. The other clans would reckon that with the king's backing they in turn could raid the Clan Donald lands and gain rich booty themselves. But Campbell was a clever man and thought of a further, truly devious twist.

By now John, Lord of the Isles, had negotiated his freedom again. Argyll got in touch with him, and we can imagine just what he was saying. It seems he told John that Angus Og was becoming so powerful that he was even a threat to his own father. As an illegitimate son it was unlikely he would ever get the chance to succeed John as Lord of the Isles but if he gathered a sufficient number of men and defeated a sufficient number of the other clans he could effectively take over all of the lands that were rightfully his father's. Whether this was ever part of Angus Og's plan we can never really know, but it was such a feasible idea that John was lured into giving his support to Campbell. So they got together a great fleet of birlinns, the traditional west-coast galleys, and met Angus's force in a sea-battle off the point of Ardnamurchan. This sea-battle has come down to us as the Battle of Bloody Bay, and despite the best efforts of the Camp-bells and the MacDonalds under John's leadership, once again Angus Og was triumphant. Was there nothing that could stop him?

After the battle he took the opportunity to ravage the lands of northern Argyll, and flushed with success he ventured east in to Atholl to carry on the harrying. Angus had a bone or two to pick with the Earl of Atholl. Apart from his role in capturing Angus's father the Earl had earlier managed to abduct Angus's infant son, Donald Dubh, and had given him into the keeping of the boy's maternal grandfather, the Earl of Argyll. The wee lad was in fact kept for many years as a prisoner in the Castle of Inchconnelly. By now Angus Og and his men were doing as they pleased without hindrance, and they must have thought that nothing could stop them. When they got to Atholl they found that the Earl and the Countess were hiding in the Chapel of St Bride, close to Blair Castle.

Undeterred by the fact that they had entered the chapel to claim sanctuary, Angus Og burst into the church and took them prisoner. He reckoned that many would be planning vengeance against him after his remarkable campaign and that the Earl and Countess would make good hostages in any forthcoming nego-tiations with the king. Now this made a great deal of sense, but fate, and perhaps Highland superstition, stepped in to change matters. Angus and his followers returned to the west coast with their hostages and a phenomenal amount of booty – gold, silver, weapons and domestic chattels, as well as vast herds of cattle. There they met up with the birlinn fleet, and, as the weather seemed fair, if overcast, they embarked to sail back to Islay. They were hardly out into the open sea before a great storm blew up as if out of nowhere. There was nothing they could do. The howling winds and raging seas drove them back to the mainland

and more than a few of the booty-laden birlinns went to the bottom of the sea with their crews.

When the bedraggled and battered Highlanders were safe on land their thoughts turned to what had happened.

'We should never have broken the rules of sanctuary. This is St Bride's way of telling us,' said one old veteran to Angus.

'Aye, great Bride has turned her face against us because of what we have done against her in her own chapel,' put in another. Within minutes these fierce Highland warriors who had just conquered nearly half of Scotland and defeated clan after clan were awestricken and remorseful over taking two people prisoner!

However, Bride was considered of particular importance. The Highlanders reckoned her to have been miraculously transported to Bethlehem to help in the birth of Christ, and even before the word of the Christians had come amongst them Bride had been a goddess of rebirth and renewal. Even these supposedly good Christians were not free of the ancient beliefs of their fathers when it came to the power of Bride. To them it was more than likely that she had directly intervened because of this insult given to her by Angus's capture of the Atholls! And the one most affected by this belief? Angus Og himself! He now believed he was cursed by his own actions, and the decisive and brilliant military leader of just a few days before was replaced by a man racked with self doubt and a sense of imminent doom. At once he released the Atholls, sending them back with an escort, and began to plan a sad return to his island home. He never made it. Just before he was about to embark on his journey home Angus Og was slain by his own harper!

A Dish Best Served Cold

⟫⟩◆⟨⟪

The Well of the Seven Heads

Donald Glas, the 12th chief of the Clan Ronald, the MacDonalds of Keppoch, was a far-seeing man. In the middle of the seventeenth century he followed the practice of many of the clan chiefs of his time and sent his eldest son Alexander, with his brother Ranald, to the Continent to be educated. Like many of the Highland chiefs, Donald Glas was a Catholic and had sent his sons to Rome to be taught by the priests there. The Highland clans might have held on to a way of life that had its roots back in the Iron Age but they were never unsophisticated or ignorant savages. Donald himself died while the lads were still in Rome and the clan was looked after by his brother Alexander Buidhe on behalf of his nephew, and he took the title of Clan Tutor, there being nothing unusual in this. The plan was that Alexander Buidhe's nephew would become chief of the clan when he was old enough.

Alex and Ranald came back from their studies and soon afterwards a great feast was held for Alex's investiture as the thirteenth chief of the Keppoch MacDonalds. The investiture of a new chief was always the opportunity for a great feast which was held in the great hall of the main house at Keppoch, where the most important guests were gathered round a great table. Among them were a father and his six sons, from Inverlair in Glen Roy, known as the Siol Dughaill. Now they were friends of Alexander Buidhe, and in fact had two of his sons with them at the feast. In the course of the banquet they started a fight. Their plan was simple. Start the fight, get as many people involved as possible – never difficult among Highland warriors with their highly developed sense of individual honour and consequent pride – and ensure that both Alexander and his brother Ronald would be killed in the ensuing melee.

Their treacherous plan worked perfectly, and when at last the fighting stopped the new chief and his brother lay dead on the floor of their own home! The Siol Dughaill were to the fore in lamenting this dreadful deed. The story was put out that it had been an unfortunate and tragic mistake. It had been no more than a truly dreadful accident that this had happened, but such things often resulted from warriors drawing their swords; everyone knew that!

Alexander Buidhe had to carry on as temporary chief, and from that time onwards there were rumours circulating that he himself might even have had a hand in this nasty piece of work. The Siol Dughaill returned home to await developments after the new chief and his brother were buried with all due honour.

There was one man however who was certain that this had been no accident and he determined not to wait around. Iain Lom, the bard of Keppoch, was in no doubt that the whole thing had been a set-up and he well knew who was to blame. Vengeance was called for, and immediately after the funeral he went to see one of the other MacDonald chiefs, MacDonald of Glengarry. In his house at Invergarry Iain Lom asked him to help him take revenge on these kin-slayers.

'Well now Iain,' said Glengarry, 'I am not as sure as you that this was deliberate. After all hasn't Alisdair Buidhe himself said we should let things calm down for a while?'

'That is as may be, but my chief and his brother are dead and buried. They were killed by men of their own clan. This must be revenged. Will you help me or not?' demanded the vengeful poet.

'Well, with Alisdair wanting to let things settle down, I think in the circumstances I'll let things lie for a while Iain,' came the reply.

Iain Lom was disgusted at this refusal to do what he clearly saw was required, and he stormed off from Invergarry. However, he was not the sort of man to give up on anything once he had started. Next he went to Skye and asked to see MacDonald of Sleat. The chief was pleased to see Iain, whose fame as both a bard and a warrior made him a man of some standing within his community. He was happy to listen to the famous bard and their conversation has been passed down.

'Where have you come from?' enquired James of Sleat.

'From Laodicea,' came the reply. This was a biblical reference to the church at Laodicea which was criticised for being lukewarm in putting forth the Christian word, and it is a fair reflection of the literacy and sophistication of educated clansmen of the time that James understood the reference. Iain was saying that Glengarry was not ready to act. But James agreed at once to help Iain Lom bring the murderers to justice. He was no fool though, and before giving Iain direct help to pursue the Inverlair men and their friends, he went to the Privy Council and asked for a commission to bring the murderers of the young chief and his brother to justice. This, he hoped, would help to prevent any further troubles arising from Iain's actions. Using the government to support their actions was a regular ploy by some of the Highland chiefs, though in the long run it could only help to diminish their own authority and undermine the traditional ways of clan life. The commission was given on 29 June, 1665, and it is striking that two of the men named in the commission were Alan Dearg and his brother Donald, sons of Alexander Buidhe, Tutor of the Clan!

Once the commission had been granted James gave Iain fifty clansmen to accompany him to Inverlair, under the command of James's own brother Archibald, like Iain a renowned Gaelic bard. Four days after leaving Sleat the Skye contingent arrived at Inverlair. News of their approach had gone ahead of them and the Sioll Dughaill and their friends had gathered at Inverlair and barricaded themselves in the house there.

Of Alexander Buidhe's sons there was no sign; Alan Dearg and Donald had left the country and it was many years before the latter returned. Alan never did come back to Scotland, which perhaps tells us all we need to know about his part in the original crime!

Seven of the original gang however were indoors when the Sleat contingent arrived and attacked the house.

There was a great deal of shooting to begin with, and the men in the house gave a good account of themselves by killing more than a few of their attackers. After a few hours of this, Iain was becoming frustrated.

'We'll just have to burn them out,' he said to Archibald. So under the cover of a series of volleys a couple of the Skye men ran into the house and threw burning brands onto the roof. Like most Highland houses of the time the roof was mainly thatched with heather, and once it caught fire it blazed fiercely. There was no way the men inside the house could survive as the burning heather and roof timbers began to crash down on them. Sputtering and coughing they charged out from the inferno, there to die on the swords of their attackers who greatly outnumbered them.

Standing there over the seven corpses as the house blazed fiercely behind him, Iain knew what he had to do. Taking a dirk from one of the corpses – a dirk that it seems had itself been used in the murder of the young chief – he proceeded to cut the heads off all of the seven corpses. Putting the heads into a large sack he hoisted it over his shoulder, and leaving the Skye men to bury those they had lost the fight, he immediately set out for Sleat. On his way he passed along the western shore of Loch Oich, nowadays a part of the Caledonian Canal. There, at a well by the side of the road close to Ardrishaig, north of Laggan, he took out the heads of the seven murderers and carefully washed the blood off them. This was a symbolic act to rebuke Glengarry for his refusal to support Iain in his search for justice. He then headed straight to Sleat where he presented the heads to James, who then sent them off to Edinburgh to the Privy Council as proof of the execution of his commission. The well on the Loch Oich shore was known ever after as the Well of the Seven Heads and nowadays incorporates a sculpture of seven severed heads as part of its structure. Back in the seventeenth century though, even though Iain Lom had his revenge on some of the murderers at least, no one was really surprised when Alexander Buidhe was confirmed as head of the clan a few years later.

An Eye for an Eye

For many centuries there was great deal of tension between the Scottish monarchs and the warrior tribes of Scotland. While today most people are aware of the clans of Highland Scotland, there were other areas where the writ of the court was largely seen as an irrelevance. In the Border area with England and in the wilds of Dumfries and Galloway men were just as liable to go about armed and ready for trouble as they were in the Highlands up until the Middle Ages. Even the idea of Scotland itself was not really very important to many of the armed warriors. Such people saw their right to live as they wished on their own lands as something that had come down from time immemorial. Kings saw matters differently, especially after David I, who tried so hard to impose something like the feudal system of England on his country. In truth, Scotland was never really feudal, even if the kings did love to hand out charters and give titles to their aristocratic favourites. What mattered most was having a good crowd of men who could fight at your beck and call. This the chiefs of the clans certainly had.

But these warriors were raised to think for themselves, and though the ties of blood and loyalty to kinfolk were supreme, they were never soldiers to be commanded; they were warriors who, though they would gladly die for their chief, were in no way his vassals. They were all Highland gentlemen. So it was that some of the habits of the kings of Scotland went directly against the grain of what many saw to be their traditional way of life, though that is not how they would have put it. One of the problems that regularly arose throughout the Middle Ages was the policing of the King's Forests. These were not plantations grown for profit like the monotonous monoculture that blights so much of our landscape these days, but areas, mainly of wood-land, which were reserved for hunting. The main targets were of course deer, though a couple of centuries earlier the fierce wild boar had often been hunted. In fact it was probably the popu-larity of hunting that led to the extinction of the wild boar in Scotland. Hunting was something in which traditionally all levels of society participated. There is an old saying to the effect that taking a deer from the hill, a salmon from the river and fuel from the woods are three crimes of which a Highlander can never be convicted. This is a reference to the truly ancient ways of hunting and foraging on the land that originate from the time when humans first came settle in this island of ours. Kings, though, saw things differently.

Increasingly, kings from David I onwards, thought that they and not the people owned the land, a concept that soon passed down to their so-called aristocratic relatives and friends. In time the clan chiefs too grasped this concept with both hands! And so it was that vast areas of the country were designated as forest or hunting areas set aside for the king's pleasure. There are those who will still tell you that hunting is some kind of aristocratic activity, while all the evidence shows that hunting, for the pot, played a substantial part in the diet of many Scots throughout the Middle Ages. Hunting for pleasure was a different thing entirely, and the kings cared little for the traditional practices of their so-called subjects. One of them, King James VI, a man who, when the chance came for him to turn his back on Scotland couldn't be seen for dust, was particularly jealous of his hunting rights.

He particularly liked hunting in the Forest of Glen Artney, to the south-west of the modern town of Comrie. Now in order to look after his hunting grounds James had appointed a forester. This was John Drummond of Drummond Ernoch, who, like many others over the centuries, was glad to seek the patronage of the monarch. He took his job seriously – perhaps too seriously. One day while patrolling the forest with a large group of his men he came across three MacGregors. Now the MacGregors were long the object of persecution, and were effectively outlaws. Until recently it was the belief of Highlanders that just as they could plough the land to grow oats to make porridge, and barley to make their own whisky, so the fruits of the land like deer and other animals were just another aspect of God's bounty. They had no respect at all for the idea that the deer in this part of Scotland belonged to the king; the game laws were anathema to them.

That day the MacGregors had shot a deer and were busy gralloching – disembowelling – it when Drummond and a group of his men found them. The MacGregors, heavily outnumbered, looked up to see themselves surrounded by Drummonds. At pistol-point they allowed themselves to be disarmed by Drummond's men. Their attitude might well have been that there was no point in getting into a fight that they were guaranteed to lose over a deer. Drummond, however, saw things differently. Once the Gregorach had been disarmed things took a sinister turn. Drummond had them all securely tied up. He then proceeded to have their ears cut off before escorting them to the edge of the forest and turning them loose, without of course giving them back their weapons. This was a terrible insult to the MacGregors. They were branded for life and would carry the shame of that day with them as long as they lived, or certainly till they had had their revenge! They might have been the target of royal persecution, but they were a fierce and noble people and there was no way that such an insult could be allowed to stand. It wasn't just the lads who had been deprived of their ears who felt insulted, it was all of their kin.

When they got back to their own lands on the Braes of Balquhidder the news spread like wildfire. Over the next few days the story was repeated over and over again, and it was agreed unanimously amongst the Gregorach that something had to be done about the King's Forester. As ever, the fact that he was one of the king's men meant little to the MacGregors. The king's writ only ever ran sporadically in the Highlands and the loyalty of the MacGregors was to their own kin, not to some distant king. So it was that a few weeks after the ear-cutting incident a group of McGregors, led by the victims of that fateful day, came under cover of night to hunt Drummond Ernoch.

They came through the forest like ghosts till they found the forester and his companions. Drummond never had a chance when the MacGregors attacked. However, once he had been killed things took an odd turn. In the far distant past it was not unknown for tribal warriors to cut off the heads of their enemies and take them home with them as trophies. By this time it was more often done to provide proof that an agreed act – whether it was execution or murder depended on your particular viewpoint – had been carried out, whether at the king's behest or on behalf of some chief or clan. Whatever the reason, the MacGregors took Drummond's head and set off for their home. Their journey took them past Ardvorlich. Now Stewart of Ardvorlich, with whom they had often been at odds, had married John Drummond's sister, and the MacGregors were aware of this and decided to play a rather cruel joke.

A handful of them came to the door of Stewart's home and

asked for some food. Mrs Stewart, who was close to giving birth at the time, had no inkling of what they had been doing, and true to the spirit of Highland hospitality, brought them into the house and put bread and cheese on the table before them, inviting them to sit and eat. One of them then asked for a drink of water, and Mrs Stewart went out to fetch a jug for him. When she came back, there on the table, with its mouth stuffed full of bread and cheese, was the head of her brother! She let out a dreadful scream, dropped the pitcher in her hands and fled from the house. The MacGregors thought this a great joke, and wrapping up the head in a plaid they resumed their journey back home. Mrs Stewart, however, ran off into the hills, where she was found much later by a search-party sent out by her husband. She was babbling incoherently and never returned to sanity after that dreadful day. It was shortly after she was brought home from the hills that she gave birth to a healthy boy, John, a man known in later life for having a wild temper and a visceral hatred of all MacGregors.

The head of Drummond was taken to the kirk at Balquhidder, and one by one all the MacGregor men, led by Alistair of Glenstrae, their chief, came and placed their hands on the forester's head, swearing to defend those who had killed the forester and defied the king.

What the MacGregors had not known was that on the day of that fateful meeting with John Drummond, the forester had been on a specific mission for his king, He was out hunting for venison for the upcoming marriage of the king to Princess Anne of Denmark – for what would a Scottish royal wedding feast have been without Scottish venison! So when Drummond was killed James took it as a personal insult, and it was this deed that finally caused the whole MacGregor clan to be outlawed, though truth to tell, James VI was following in well-worn footsteps in his persecution of the Gregorach.

191

The Night is the Night

In Loch Earn there is an island called Neish Island after one of
the clans who used to live in the glens along the north shore of
Loch Earn – the Clan Neish or the MacNeishes. The island itself
is a crannog or artificial island, a type of dwelling common in
Scottish lochs, some of them thousands of years old. The
Neishes were possibly a sept, or sub-clan, of the unfortunate
MacGregors, and had a reputation as a troublesome bunch. As
far back as 1490 James IV had ordered that their castle on the isle
be 'cast doon' and all boats there destroyed. This was done, but
some of the Neishes lived on amidst the ruins of the fortalice.
While inter-clan raiding was a normal aspect of clan life the
Neishes seem to have been more like professional robbers and
were considered little more than criminals by their neighbours.

One of the nearby clans, the Macnabs, who held the lands
round the south-eastern part of Loch Tay had an ongoing feud
with the Neishes for many, many years. The origins of the clan
feud are lost in the mists of time, but at last a great battle was
fought in 1522 between the two clans near the present farm of
Littleport in Glenboltachan. In this fight the MacNabs were led
by their chief, Finlay. The two clans rushed down the green
slopes of the hills to close in hand-to hand fighting, with wild
yells and curses, while their war-cries rang out.

Eventually the MacNabs bore all before them, and the aged
chief of the Neishes, having seen the heart-rending sight of three
of his sons fall by his side, was forced to set his back to a great
granite boulder, and, whirling his mighty claymore, the great
two-handed sword of the Highlands, he stood like a beast at bay.
He was a giant of a man, famous for strength and bravery even
amongst the Highland warriors, and as he stood there, towering
over his enemies, his long greying hair blowing in the wind and
blood flowing from an arrow wound on his brow, he was a
fearsome sight. His sword had a strange attachment, like an iron

ball that slid along the back of the blade as he swung the weapon and gave an additional weight to every blow. The Macnabs paused, then surged forward – more than a dozen of them – to attack the chief. Several of them died from the blows of his great swinging blade before he himself fell, pierced by more than a half a dozen swords and dirks. The red lichen that covers the boulder to this day is believed in local tradition to be the result of the blood spilt by this mighty warrior's passing. Elsewhere things were going just as badly for the rest of the Neishes. The MacNabs were totally triumphant, and only a small remnant of the MacNeishes, fewer than twenty, under the leadership of their clan bard, MacCallum Glas, managed to escape to the small island near the east end of Loch Earn.

From here they managed to carry out various raids on other clans, but such was their poverty and lack of resources that they were reduced to being little more than freebooters, stealing what they could, when they could. The situation continued for many years, the one thing that seemed to be keeping them together in their miserable life being their all-consuming hatred for the MacNabs. The MacNabs for their part thought little if anything about this bedraggled remnant of their once-powerful enemy.

In 1612, Finlay, the twelfth chief of the MacNabs, decided to have a particularly splendid feast at Christmas time. With no reason to expect any trouble on his own clan's lands, he sent just one of his clansmen to Crieff with a string of ponies to purchase everything fine that might be available in the way of food and drink. He had been prospering of late, and he wanted to show both his clan, and his neighbouring chiefs, just how generous he could be. This was pretty much in keeping with the general ostentation of Highland chiefs who, whenever possible, would show off how well they were doing – a habit that was usually supported by the members of their clans. The poorer ones would get a bit of a treat and everybody would bask in the renown that such behaviour brought to the clan. It was normal clan practice.

Somehow, the band of MacNeishes heard about the plans for this feast in advance, and were lying in ambush by the roadside as the Macnab made his way back home. He had no chance to put up a fight before he was surrounded by the Neishes pointing swords and pistols at him. He was knocked from his horse and given a severe beating before the MacNeishes made off, laughing, with their booty.

As he lay there in his own blood the Macnab called after them, 'This is not the end of things. You will pay for this yet.'

His cry was met with derisive shouts of laughter as the MacNeishes headed back to their island retreat. They were sure they were safe, as they had the only boat on Loch Earn, and once it was safely beached on their island home they fell to eating and drinking with a will. It wasn't long before they were virtually all blind drunk, many of them falling asleep where they sat in their rough wooden hall, amongst the old ruins of the castle.

When his messenger hadn't returned home at the expected time the Macnab sent out a search-party for him and they found the poor lad hirpling home in a dreadful state. He was taken immediately to his clan chief, and while his wounds were being treated he told the chief what had happened. Macnab was furious, but sat quietly pondering, all of his twelve sons and other close relatives waiting to see what he would say.

He didn't say a lot, but looking at his eldest son, a dour, scruffy, saturnine man called Smooth John in the typical Highland fashion, because of his rough appearance and even worse manners, he declared: 'The night is the night, if the lads are the lads.'

Rough and uncouth Smooth John might have been, but he caught his father's meaning immediately. He and his brothers were all big powerful men and were known for being almost unbeatable at the various athletic games that all the clans liked to hold. Without a word he signalled to his brothers to follow him, and, picking up their swords and pistols, they all went down to the shore of Loch Tay. Here they dragged a large rowing boat from the water and hoisting it on their shoulders they marched along the south bank of the loch, up the shoulders of Creag Gharbh, and over into Glen Tarkin, coming out a couple of miles from the eastern half of Loch Earn. It was winter, dark, and the weather was blustery and wet with that underlying coldness, creating the unpleasant conditions we call 'dreich'. The Macnabs did not seem to notice it. If any of his brothers had complained they knew fine well they were likely to be given more than a slap from their fierce eldest brother. So even if any had been unhappy at the situation, there was no way anything would be said. And after all, they were warriors of the Clan MacNab, as brave and strong as any man on Planet Earth, as their father had told them often enough! Once they were at the western end of Loch Earn they muffled the oars and set off at a steady pace towards the MacNeish's hideout.

They reached the island, and in absolute silence they hauled the boat onto the shore, drew their weapons and entered the rough timber building that was home to the MacNeishes. All were sound asleep except the bard who had taken the role of chief. He was restless, in a half sleep; his dreams had been full of foreboding and had wakened him a while earlier. He heard, as if in his dream, a voice asking, 'Who would you least like to be seeing at this moment, MacNeish?'

Turning over on the stamped earth floor, where he lay wrapped in his plaid, he muttered in his half-sleeping state, 'Smooth John Macnab.'

At once the answer roared: 'If he's been smooth up to now, you'll find him rough enough this night!'

MacNeish sat up straight, his eyes popping. There, in the doorway of the building stood the awesome figure of Smooth John Macnab with his brothers all behind him. He grabbed for his sword, shouting 'Awake, awake,' but the words were barely out of his throat before Smooth John fell on him. A few of the

MacNeishes came half awake but the slaughter was over in minutes. The Macnabs gathered up all the food and drink that remained, and as his brothers carried it all to the boat, Smooth John decapitated the MacNeish's chieftain and slipped the head inside his plaid before leaving the dreadful scene. The Mac-Neishes had been wiped out – a good night's work he thought. But he had not noticed that below one of the rough-hewn beds that stood against the wall opposite the door, two pairs of wide eyes had seen the carnage. A wee boy and girl had watched the awful killing spree.

Back to the boat the Macnabs went, laughing and joking amongst themselves. As always, Smooth John was silent as they rowed back to the shore. Dividing the food and drink amongst them, they once more hoisted the boat on their shoulders and advanced up Glen Tarkin. Now they were hardy Highland warriors, but they had already carried this boat many miles, rowed it out to the island and back, and besides, they were carrying a great deal of the high-class fare that the MacNeishes had stolen.

Even for them the boat became too much, and before they reached the head of Glen Tarkin, Smooth John gave the order to dump the boat. They could always come back for it another time, and if not – well, they had avenged the insult on their father and their clan, and what was the price of boat to that? By now the light was coming into the sky, and as they traversed the head of Glen Beich and reached the waters of Lochan Braechlaich they passed the home of an old woman who lived alone. She was a woman who possessed much lore of herbs and plants, was known to have the second sight and was generally thought of as something of a witch. However, she was of their own folk, and the brothers, seeing her fire was already lit, knocked on her door and offered her some of the food they were carrying. She refused.

'Why do you refuse the offer of this fancy food, mother?' asked a puzzled Smooth John.

'Beware the sons of Neish,' came the cryptic reply, 'beware of the time when there will be two boats on Loch Earn.' Saying this, she shut the door of her simple cottage up there in the hills. Somehow she knew that some Neishes had been left alive and that in years to come this could prove ominous for the Macnabs.

Smooth John simply grunted; he was not a man given to believing in anything he could not see or touch, and he and his brothers made for home.

Coming to their father's house near mid-morning they entered to find the Macnab waiting them. As he saw they were carrying the stolen goods he smiled and looked quizzically at his eldest son.

Reaching into his plaid John drew out the head of the MacNeish chieftain and simply said, 'There is nothing to worry about now,' and laughed a hard laugh.

'Well then,' said the delighted Macnab, 'the night was surely the night and the lads were surely the lads.'

And there are those who will tell you that this occasion gave rise to the Macnab Crest, a bearded head with words 'Dread Nought'!

As for the boat the MacNabs had carried over the hills, it was left to rot, and it is said that pieces of it could still be seen as late as the early nineteenth century, and some families in the area preserve walking sticks made from pieces of it. And as for the wee lad and lass who had been sleeping below the bed in the rough hall on Neish Island; well, that is another story, but there are still MacNeishes living in Scotland and elsewhere to this day.

Donald Cam Macaulay

One of the most famous of the fighting men in the islands was Donald Cam Macaulay from Uig on the west coast of Lewis. One time he and his close companion 'the Big Smith', *An Gobhan Mor*, had gone to the Flannan Isles some fifteen miles west of Lewis to catch birds. In those far-off times the sea-birds provided one of the regular sources of food, and most of the men from Uig were on the expedition. In their absence a band of Morrisons from Ness in the north of the island took advantage of the situation by visiting Uig and departing with a fair number of cattle. On returning and hearing of this from the women, Donald and a group of the Macaulays jumped back into a boat and sailed up the coast, hoping to catch up with the marauders. As they passed the island of Great Bernera in Loch Roag, near the ancient stones of Calanais, they spotted their cattle near the old broch tower of Dun Carloway [brochs are a 2000-year-old form of defensive structure unique to Scotland]. This suggested that the Morrisons were themselves probably occupying the broch itself. So, coming ashore quietly, the Macaulays rested nearby till night began to fall. Now they had left Uig in a hurry, and by now Donald and the rest of the party were very hungry indeed. So he and the Big Smith decided to creep up to the old broch to see if there was any food that they could steal. As they approached the broch they realised there was a fire burning nearby, and on it was a great iron cauldron. The man who was obviously looking after whatever was in the cauldron was lying fast asleep near the fire. It was likely that he was also supposed to be a lookout. If so, he certainly wasn't doing his job.

The pair of them went up to the fire. There in the great cauldron was the cut-up carcase of one of the cattle that had been lifted that afternoon. The rich aroma of the cooking meat made their hunger even worse. As Donald lifted the meat from the cauldron and wrapped it in his plaid, the Smith used his plaid to muffle the man on the ground, before lifting him and sticking him head first into the cauldron itself! He held him there till he stopped struggling, while Donald hoisted the meat over his shoulder and the two of them went back to where their companions were waiting. All of this was done with hardly a noise at all.

When they got back to where the others were they all fell on the meat with gusto, slicing great chunks off of the carcase with their dirks. When all had eaten sufficiently Donald told them in whispers what the plan of attack was to be. The men scattered out and began to cut bunches of heather which they tied into large bundles for carrying on their backs; they then advanced in a group towards the broch. As they approached they got down on all fours and Donald crawled towards the sentry who was lounging about at the entrance to the broch.

Now brochs were designed as defensive structures and had only one small opening in their dry-stone circular structure. The door was barely a couple of feet high, just wide enough for an adult to crawl through, and the overall shape of the broch slightly resembled the cooling towers you see at modern power stations, narrowing towards the top. Their construction meant that one man could keep a whole army at bay, and their exteriors were impervious to most forms of attack before the invention of gunpowder. But Donald knew all about the brochs and was acutely aware of what he was planning. He crept up on the sentry, who, like his companion at the fire, wasn't really keeping an eye open, and before he knew what was happening Donald attacked him and stabbed him to the heart. He signalled to the Big Smith to come up and stand at the outside of the small door with his great double-headed sword. Just as no one could get through without exposing himself, so no one could get out without falling to the Big Smith's blade.

Donald then took two dirks, and still keeping as quiet as he could he used the dirks to climb up the thirty-foot-high exterior of the broch. Once he was there he shoved aside the great stone slab that covered the top. By now the Morrisons were aware that they had arrived and he could hear them discussing what they could do. They could do nothing, he thought grimly, as he signalled for his men to start throwing up the bundles of heather. As they threw them up he caught them and dropped them down inside the broch. Bundle after bundle was thrown down as the

Morrisons tried to shoot at him. But there was no target for them to hit, as Donald was balanced on the outside of the wall and they could not climb up to attack him with a sword, the ancient wooden stairways and platforms of the old broch having long rotted away. When he judged that enough heather had been thrown in he began lighting the bundles still being thrown up to him and tossing them inside. The Morrisons stamped out a few, but soon too many of the heather bundles were alight and in the thick cloying smoke they were getting in each others' way. And all the time the Macaulays were cutting heather and making bundles to toss to Donald who kept throwing them inside the broch. Eventually the smoke became too much for the beleaguered Morrisons and to a man they suffocated there in the ancient broch of Dun Carloway.

This was not the only time that Donald Macaulay had trouble with the Morrisons. One time he, Torquil Dubh MacLeod and some others were invited aboard a ship that had been captured by John Morrison, chief of the clan. It was anchored off the north-east cost of Lewis and Donald, Torquil and the others came along in good faith expecting to have a good feed and take advantage of Morrisons's offer of hospitality. Now in those days when boarding a ship that had below decks space it was the custom to leave one's arms on the deck. This was done, and the guests went below to partake of the lavish hospitality that was on offer. They started to eat, and have a drink or two and generally enjoy the company. However, it wasn't long before Donald realised that the ship was beginning to roll. He rose from the table and went on deck to find that the cable had been slipped and that they were heading across the Minch.

'Torquil, it's a trick; we're heading across the Minch. Come now,' he shouted as he ran to where he had placed his sword, dirk and targe. They were of course nowhere to be seen, and at that the crewmen jumped him. The first to come near was a famous strongman called John Mor Mackay, and he managed to hold Donald in his grasp while others wrestled him to the mast to which they proceeded to tie him. Torquil Dubh too was seized and tied hand and foot, as were the small number of kinsmen they had with them. It soon became clear that they were heading into Ullapool.

On landing, the prisoners were taken ashore and Donald was chained by the neck and one foot to a large boulder along with his son in law Alasdair MacLeod. Now as with most Islemen, Alisdair had a nickname. The store of names in use amongst the Gaeltachd being generally very limited, each man was differentiated by the nickname. Now Alisdair was called 'Little-heel' for the simple reason that one of his feet was much smaller than the other. As luck would have it, Alisdair had been shackled round the ankle of his left and smaller foot. So as their captors went off leaving them in the open chained to the massive boulder it was a simple matter for Alisdair to slip his foot from the shackle. He then helped Donald Mor lift the massive rock onto his broad shoulders and the two of them, both still attached to the boulder, made for the hills.

They roamed north, always parallel to the shore, but coming down to the beach every so often to see if they could find a boat. Well, they found plenty of boats, but not one of them with any oars. At long last, after covering the country all the way to Applecross, with Donald carrying the great stone all the way, they had had enough. There they found a boat lying keel upwards on the sands. Now it was an old boat, and they could see the beach through the gaps and splits along its planks, it was hardly a seaworthy vessel! Luckily Alisdair had spotted some clay nearby at the edge of a burn and they carried some of that to the boat to caulk the gaps as best they could. Donald then tore a couple of lengths of wood from the gate of a sheep-fank on the nearby hill, to use as oars, and they were ready.

So they set out in the leaky boat for Skye, though Donald by now was exhausted. Carrying the great stone all that way had drained even him and he soon collapsed in a heap, leaving Alisdair to do the rowing. Stopping every so often to bail out the decrepit hulk they eventually came ashore near to Dunvegan Castle itself. Here they were warmly greeted by Alisdair's kinfolk, and it wasn't long before Donald was separated from the great burden he had carried for so many miles. The great block with its chains was kept for many years at Dunvegan Castle.

A few days later, after a good rest, the pair of them came back to Lewis, where they were met with a great welcome. Their family had been certain they would never see them again in this life, and here they were, having made a daring escape from John Morrison's clutches. Their return was the talk of the place, and it wasn't long before it came to the ears of Morrison himself who had returned to Ness.

Now Donald Cam blamed the strong man, John Mor Mackay, for his capture and was hellbent on having his revenge. Barely a week after Donald and Alisdair had made their arduous journey, Morrison and John Mackay also returned to Harris to hear the news that their foes had escaped. Fine well they knew that Donald would be planning his revenge. Morrison returned to his home and surrounded himself with as many of his kin as he could gather, while John Mor Mackay decided to hide out in the old broch on the shores of the freshwater Loch an Duna.

Hearing they were back, Donald wasted no time. It didn't take him long at all to find out where John Mackay was. Gathering together a dozen of the finest warriors amongst his kin, he sent off with them to Dun Bragir with explicit instructions to capture John Mor. The men travelled through the hours of darkness and stole a boat on the shore of Lioch an Duna in which they rowed over to the old broch. Taking as much care as they could and using muffled oars they managed to gain entry to the old fortress before John Mor could awaken. Even though they came upon him asleep, the twelve of them had a hard job with Big John before they could subdue him and tie him up securely. Once dawn came they travelled back towards Uig with their prisoner, but the journey was eventful. Just as they were fording the river Grimersta, near to Linshader, John made an escape bid. Before they could knock him out he had laid a handful of his captors low; even with his hands tied behind him, his great strength made him a fearsome warrior. So by the time they got him to Kirkibost on Great Bernera most of his captors were showing signs of wear and tear!

The following day Donald came to Kirkibost with most of the population of Uig at his back. It was not so much a trial as a simple humiliation preceding death that John Mor Mackay was subjected to. The sentence, however, was unanimous – every adult in the Uig area agreed that Mackay should be put to death for his treachery against Donald Cam. While there is little doubt that the warriors of the Highland and Island clans considered themselves to be honourable men, some of their actions were a little rich for our palates these days. It was decided that a fitting end for John Mackay would be for every one of the men there to test the sharpness of their swords on him! The condemned man was taken to the Cnocan nami-Chomhairle, 'the Hillock of Ill-Advice' – which name in itself suggests some kind of rebuke – there to be subjected to his sentence.

However something was wrong. Try as they might, the Macaulays could not stick their swords in John Mor. He seemed to be made of iron. Clearly the man had some kind of magical powers, but no one knew what they were. Even more than a thousand years after the Christian religion came to Scotland we should remember that many of the truly ancient spiritual beliefs of the old pagan ways survived in the Highlands, so those who were possessed of ancient lore were asked what to do. All were stumped! Nobody had heard of anything like this before. Now John's fate had been decided, and it would not have been regarded as fair either to hang or to shoot him. He had to die by the points of the swords. All day discussions raged as to what would be the best way to weaken his magic protective powers, but nothing worked. Nothing that is, till one old woman, steeped in the knowledge of days gone by, suggested that they remove the turf from beneath his feet and make him stand on the bare earth. This was done, and the next man to try his sword on John Mor Mackay met no resistance at all – the charm was gone.

So John Mackay died to avenge the indignity and insult to Donald Cam and Alisdair Little-heel Macaulay.

Stickability

Now down the centuries the Highland warriors were famous for bravery and for never giving in. They were also known for their capacity to keep feuds going, and two of the clans who often seemed to come to blows were the Gunns from the north of Helmsdale in Sutherland and their neighbours to the south of the river, the Keiths. In 1478, while parleying with a group of Keiths, George Gunn of Cromer had been killed. In most tribal societies there were traditions and practices that came into play in such situations. In order to settle matters a battle was organised. As all Highland warriors prided themselves on their sense of honour it was decided that a battle would be fought between the two clans with twelve men on each side. This was according to an old tradition that was known as *cothrom na Feinne*, 'the fair play of the Fianna', which it was believed had been instituted by the legendary figure of Finn MacCoul.

The men of the clans were warriors, not soldiers, and the chiefs and captains who commanded them well understood that they could not command their men to do anything that they themselves were not ready to do. The leaders needed the support of their clansmen just as much as their clansmen needed the leadership they provided.

However, human nature is human nature, and the honour code of the Highland warrior did not always apply, for there is always somebody prepared to bend the rules to gain an advantage. This applied even in a society where the idea of honour was of central importance.

And so it proved that day in Sutherland. The battle had been organised to take place at Drummoy. Twelve men from each clan were to arrive on horseback and do battle. At the appointed hour the Gunns were already there when they saw the Keiths approaching, led by Keith of Ackergill. Just as had been agreed, there were twelve horses, but as the contingent grew nearer the Gunns realised that on the back of each of the approaching horses there was not one pair of legs but two! With such a numerical advantage the Keiths were certain of victory, and when they had reduced the number of the Gunns to only four they decided they had done enough to win the day. The Gunns, fired-up with the treachery of the Keiths, had fought like berserkers, and though they were now reduced to four seriously wounded men, the Keiths had suffered badly at their hands and only nine of them still breathed. As the chieftain of the Gunns was among the dead, the chief of the Keiths was satisfied, and withdrew from the battle, leaving the four wounded Gunns on the field. It was often the custom for clansmen to withdraw from the battle on the death of a chief, to give him a proper burial and appoint his successor. The remaining Gunns however, had other things on their mind besides the burial of either their chief or the rest of their companions: an honourable burial would have to wait.

They had been treated treacherously and were bent upon having their revenge. Stopping only long enough to help each other bind up their wounds they swore on their dirks – the strongest oath any Highlander could make – that they would hunt the Keiths down till either all of them or all of the devious enemy were dead! They took some food and went off in pursuit of the Keiths. Ackergill, his son and their seven companions were all wounded to some extent but were unaware that they were being tailed by the surviving Gunns. They believed they had won a notable victory over their ancient enemies, and given their condition, they decided to take it easy on their journey home.

This proved to be a costly mistake, for, despite their wounds the Gunns managed to creep through the low-lying hills of Sutherland and get ahead of the Keiths. Passing the enemy, they crept along the side of a hill and lay in ambush at a narrow spot in the road. Just as Ackergill and his men came to the spot, the Gunns leapt out of the heather with all the advantage of surprise. The struggle was short and fierce, and within a matter of minutes two more of the Gunns lay dead. Their deaths though had been at a grave price to the Keiths. Ackergill rode off with only three companions, including his son, and now they were all as badly hurt as the two surviving Gunns. The onslaught of the Gunns had killed five of their enemies! Of the two remaining Gunns, one lay as if dead amongst the bodies of his enemies, while his companion had run off into the heather when he realised he was on his own. He returned once Ackergill had left, and finding one of his cousins alive he soon revived him. They were still not finished! Again they swore to have revenge, and despite their extensive wounds and blood-loss they resumed their pursuit of the Keiths.

Not long after this the Keiths stopped to bathe and treat their wounds at a ford in a burn below a large overhanging rock. As they did so, the last two Gunns crept up the rock and launched themselves amongst their enemy, each man lashing out with his sword in one hand and his dirk in the other. Such was their fury that the Keiths were struck down to a man. There, amongst the bodies of their enemies, the two Gunns lay, incapable of moving, their recent actions having drained them of all their energy, and sure in their hearts that they would die there on the hillside. Never mind that though, they had avenged the treachery of the devious Keiths, and none of them would return home to crow about how they had fooled the men of Clan Gunn. All through the long night they lay there, unable to help each other and getting weaker with each passing hour.

It wasn't long after dawn when some of their fellow clansmen who had followed their trail from Drummoy found them. Taking great care of them they bandaged up their wounds, fed them broth and took them back over the hills on litters dragged by horses. It was a tough journey, but at last they got back to their homes to be treated as heroes. Once they had recovered from their miraculous actions both of them survived to live to a ripe old age.

The Chief who Asked too Much

The cateran raiding of the clans, where an armed band would set out from one clan to lift the cattle of some distant tribe, was a practice rooted in the far past. Roman historians drew attention to the pleasure that the Picts and Caledonians took in raiding when the Pax Romana ruled over England. There are even some historians who see the great Barbarian Conspiracy of AD 360, when the Picts, Scots and visiting Saxons stormed over Hadrian's Wall and ravaged almost the whole of England, as little more than a gigantic raid. There can be no doubt that raiding was 'in the blood' of the Highland clans. In 1341 John Munro had been out following the habits of his ancestors, and was returning from Perthshire with a good *creach*, or spoil. On the way home to Easter Ross he had to pass through Strathspey, Clan Chattan territory. In those days, when clans raided other clan's cattle there were all sorts of rules and traditions, and in some cases obligations. One of these was the payment of a road-collop, or a percentage of the booty, for convoying the lifted cattle through another clan's lands. This of course diminished the number of cattle but helped to ensure that you would get home, because once the road-collop was paid the recipients were honour-bound to delay any pursuit from the people originally raided.

Having come through Strathspey the Munroes entered the Mackintosh lands near Loch Moy. Munro was met by none other than the Mackintosh himself, the chief of the clan and titular leader of the whole of Clan Chattan. They stood some way off from the herd, with just a couple of men each in attendance. John offered what he thought was a reasonable amount, but Mackintosh insisted that he wanted half of the booty.

'Half!' snorted Munro, 'Aye, that'll be right. Do you think we are fools to lightly hand over so much of what we have worked so hard for? You are getting nothing. Do your worst Mackintosh,' and saying this Munro turned away, signalling his men to move the herd on.

The Mackintoshes' hands all went to their sword hilts, but there were far too many Munroes and only the three of them, so their swords remained undrawn. That would not be the case for long though, thought the furious Mackintosh chief.

'Right lads, you know what to do,' he said, as he turned and strode off towards the nearest clachan. His companions at once ran off in opposite directions. Munro hardly spared them a glance but several of his men noted what had happened. They also knew what to expect next.

If the road-collop had been paid, and it would have been, had the Mackintosh not been so imperious in his demands, the Mackintoshes would have been honour-bound to prevent pursuit, even if it meant they had to fight to do it. They would have been perfectly ready to fight any band sent off to chase the Munroes, and if some of them lost their lives, well, that was just the way of things for a Highland warrior. But they had been insulted, so now their fighting skills would be brought to bear against the Munroes. Such were the niceties of the Highland clansmen's highly developed sense of honour, though here they were surely complicated by a bit too much chiefly pride.

As the Munroes headed north with their booty, behind them the *crann-tara* was sent around the Mackintosh lands and within an hour or so a large band of men had gathered. Mackintosh looked at his men and realised that the numbers were not as great as he had hoped. Many of the Mackintosh men were off raiding themselves, something he had not taken into consideration when making his ill-fated demands. Still, Munro had insulted him and that could not be let pass. So the Mackintoshes set off at a trot, following the clear trail of the cattle herd.

They caught up with the Munroes at Clachnaharry, in the shadows of the hill fort of Craig Phadrig in modern Inverness. The Munroes were expecting them and had been keeping a lookout. By the time the Mackintoshes came up John Munro had sent the herd on ahead with a skeleton crew of the youngest lads and was waiting with the rest of his men.

The battle was fought with swords and axes. The vicious brutality of hand-to-hand combat was something all those men were trained for, and in the circumstances, one side protecting what they saw as their legitimate spoil and the others seeking to avenge an insult addressed to them on their own lands, there would be little or no quarter asked or given. Whenever the Highland clans battled the chance of a great deal of bloodshed was considerable. And so it proved that day. As night fell and the John Munro led his kin home with their booty they left behind them a good few of their nearest relations along with a considerable number of Mackintoshes lying dead on the field at Clachnaharry. The latter group included the chief who had asked too much. To this day a stone memorial, badly damaged in a storm, stands to mark the spot where this avoidable but all too predictable battle took place.

The Well of the Head

There was an ancient practice in clan society whereby a family that had suffered the death of a male would be subject to the *each-ursainn*, the fine of a horse; or if no horse was available the best cow belonging to the family would do. Now this practice had originated in the distant past when the number of fighting men available to the clan was of the utmost importance and the loss of a warrior to the clan was a serious thing. This loss was made up to some extent supposedly by presenting a horse to the chief as a contribution towards the fighting strength of the clan as a whole. However, by late clan times this ancient practice had become little more than a device for unscrupulous chiefs to enrich themselves at the expense of their most defenceless clansfolk. One such chief was MacKinnon of Strath in Skye. Unlike his ancestors who well understood the responsibilities of the chief to all of the people of his clan, MacKinnon saw his status as an opportunity for self-aggrandisement and for lining his own pockets.

In this he was ably assisted by the ground-officer, a position that combined the functions of tax-collector and policeman. This was a man called Donachadh Mor, a man as lacking in true Highland virtue as MacKinnon himself – a bully, and if truth be told, little more than a legitimised thug! One time, on the death of a man in Strath, Donnachadh Mor arrive to take away the man's horse from his widow. She resisted, since she was in a bad enough condition, being left on her own, without the chief and his henchman making things worse. But Donnachadh Mor was not to be gainsaid, and when the woman tried to hang onto her horse he threw her to the ground and swore at her. Now in the Highlands it was always considered the height of bad manners to treat women roughly. All knew that the MacKinnon had turned his back on traditional clan practice where the poor and needy were looked after, but the lifting of a hand against a woman was something much worse.

Donnachadh Mor was unaware that a person who had witnessed his ill-treatment of the woman was one Lachlan MacKinnon. Such was Donnachadh Mor's temperament that he would not have bothered had he seen him or not. But Lachlan knew the boorish ground-officer all too well. Lachlan's father had died when he was just a baby, and he had been told that his mother had received just the same kind of harsh treatment at the hands of Donnachadh Mor at the time.

He had grown up hating Donnachadh Mor and had long been looking for a reason to have his revenge for the hardship suffered by his mother. Now was the time, he thought, well aware of the contempt that the people of Strath had for the chief's bullying henchman.

As the ground-officer turned to lead off with the horse he found himself face to face with Lachlan. In his right hand the young man held a sword and on his left arm was a targe, the traditional shield of the Highland fighting man, with its metal-studded leather over a round wooden base, and a long spike sticking from the boss at its centre.

Donnachadh Mor's sword was in its scabbard and on his back he carried his own targe.

'What are you standing there for boy? I am on the chief's business. Get out of my way,' the older man snarled.

'No, I don't think so,' replied Lachlan in a calm voice, 'I think you should just give Effic her horse back and be about your business.'

'Why, you insolent young dog,' shouted the ground-officer, drawing his sword, and dropping the horse's reins he whipped his targe from over his shoulder and shoved his left arm into its grips. 'I have told you already I am on the business of MacKinnon himself: now get out of my way if you know what is good for you.'

Now Donnachadh Mor was, as his name indicates, a big man, but he was at heart a coward, and had never fought with anyone whom he wasn't sure he could beat – easily. His blustering was to try and overawe the younger man, whom he recognised as a fit and healthy warrior. He also had a calm air about him, and Donnachadh Mor had been around long enough to recognise that here was formidable opponent. By now a crowd had begun to form around them, several of them being men who also were carrying swords.

'Now see here,' Donnachadh Mor called, 'I am on the business of MacKinnon himself and this whippersnapper is interrupting me in my lawful business. If you people do not restrain him here and now it will go bad for all of you.'

At that he looked around the gathered crowd. Nobody said a word and nobody made a move, They were all waiting for the fight to start. Realising that he would get no help the older, bigger man made a sudden lunge at Lachlan, hoping to catch him off guard. There was little chance of that, as Lachlan parried the blow and swung at Donnachadh's head. The fight was short, if furious, as the ground-officer tried to overwhelm the youngster with an all-out fierce attack. But though he was the bigger man, Lachlan had the advantage of speed and agility and within minutes it was obvious which way the fight was going. Donnachadh Mor's attack petered out and he began to be forced back by Lachlan. The bully had not fought hand-to-hand in many a year, relying on having help any time he got into trouble, and he began to weaken. His sword arm began to grow tired and his left arm hurt with the heavy blows he was taking on his shield,

'Some of you stop him,' he shouted, as he began to understand his true situation. He might have been the chief's man, but no one would step in, and it was a matter of only a few minutes more before his shield arm weakened, allowing Lachlan a clear blow straight into his heart! The bully gave a deep sigh and fell dead to the ground. There was murmur of approval from the gathered crowd, all of whom had long despised the bully. One or two of the warriors made a clear show of coming over to Lachlan and patting him on the shoulder. It had been a fair fight and they were making it clear that they saw nothing amiss in his actions. Then Lachlan approached the body, laid down his targe and, taking hold of the hair on the back of Donnachadh Mor's head, he cut off the head with a single stroke of his sword. He then strolled calmly to the nearby well, where he washed the blood from the head before taking it home and keeping it as souvenir. The MacKinnon, on hearing what had happened and that the fight had been witnessed by a large crowd who were all on Lachlan's side, decided, as bullies often do, that discretion was the better part of valour and the *each-ursainn* was never heard of again in Strath. And ever since that day the people of Strath have called the well 'Tobar a 'Chin', the Well of the Head.

A Gentle Giant

John MacIntosh was the son of a famous father of the same name, known far and wide as McCombie Mor. They lived at Forther in Glenisla in north-east Perthsire in the seventeenth century and the father had a great reputation for dealing with caterans, or cattle-raiders from other clans. In fact for the last twenty or so years of his life, he was never bothered by raiders, though there were troubles closer to home. McCombie Mor was a giant of a man and his first-born son was hewn from the same stuff. Now the son was raised to handle weapons like all other Highland boys in those days, and along with his strength it was obvious that he had a natural athleticism and fast reflexes. In fact he seemed the very epitome of what a Highland warrior should be. His father however, had his doubts, for Young John, though intelligent and hardworking, was of a particularly gentle disposition. He was slow to anger, never held a grudge and was prone to use argument where his father would have instantly used his fists, or worse. No matter how much the old man remonstrated with his son to be more aggressive, Young John would just smile at his father and shake his head. McCombie Mor decided that something had to be done.

One night Young John was making his way back over the hills from Glenshee when he was set upon by an armed man. The surroundings were very dark, with only the stars to give light, and John was forced to draw his sword and defend himself against a spirited attack from this stranger who had appeared as if from nowhere. Not a word was said by the man, who he soon realised was every bit as big and as strong as himself. They were well matched, and the struggle continued for a good while there on the hillside. However, at last Young John began to sense that his opponent was weakening. It was no more than a faint feeling, but he increased his attack and drove his assailant back. Thrusting and swinging even harder he got the man back on his heels and continued pushing him back on the rough ground. At last the man, parrying the sword-thrust furiously, lost his footing and fell his length in the heather, At once the point of a sword was at his throat.

'Well now,' said John, between great gulps of air, 'who are you and what are you doing attacking me like this?'

The man on the ground was gulping great breaths of air and could not speak, while John stood silently over him, his sword still poised before his adversary's throat, when the prone figure managed a grunt.

'Och, John . . .' the voice came.

'Father? What in the name of some big hoose are you doing?' John dropped his sword and helped McCombie Mor to his feet.

'Ach, lad, I should never have doubted you. I just wasn't sure you were a real McCombie. I know now. You are the first man ever to best me in a fight and I salute you son,' the old man said, as he slowly got his breath back.

'You are mad, Father. I could have killed you twice,' John cried, 'and what would have happened then?'

'Ach well, you didn't,' came the gruff reply, 'you are certainly a chip off the old block. Now let's be getting home.'

From then on McCombie Mor never doubted his son again but he had maybe been right about the son's inclination to peacefulness.

For many years McCombie had been feuding with his neighbour, Robert Farquharson of Broughdearg in Glenshee. There had been several run-ins between them, and they were in almost permanent dispute over the lands of Caenlochan to the north of Glenisla. It had started many years before, when Farquharson had proposed to, and been accepted by McCombie's daughter, only to drop her for what he considered a better match. Over the years blood had been spilt and hostages taken, but both had at different times thought to use the law to their advantage. In 1672 Farquharson drove off some of MacCombie Mor's cattle that he had been grazing on Caenlochan, and the latter raised an action before the Sheriff of Forfar against his old adversary.

The case was due to be held before the Sheriff, Alexander Strachan, on 28 January, 1673. Farquharson sent word to Strachan that he would appear in person to answer all the charges, and when he heard this, MacCombie decided to send his sons, all fully armed, to Forfar to see that justice was done.

Somehow, as they came to the outskirts of Forfar, the Farquharsons were told that the court had risen and they decided to turn back home. The MacCombie brothers reached Forfar minutes later by another road, only to hear that the Farquharsons hadn't shown up at the court. This was a chance Mac-Combie didn't want to miss. Insisting that Strachan the Sheriff accompany them so that they would be acting within the law, they set off to pursue the Farquharsons. They caught up with them on the lands of Drumgley on the other side of Forfar Loch. Strachan called on Farquharson to surrender himself to the power of the court. Seeing that Strachan had Young John McCombie and his brothers with him Farquharson saw little sense in doing that, and he refused. At that, Strachan uttered the ominous phrase 'I herby brak my wand o peace.' This gave the MacCombies the right to capture him, and Young John, wanting to prevent bloodshed, ran after the fleeing Farquharson and wrapped him up in his mighty arms. He meant him no further harm, but at that point Farquharson's two brothers, John and Alexander, ran back, and, raising their pistols they shot Young John dead on the spot. As Robert MacCombie ran to try and help his brother he too was shot down. The rest of the brothers then came up and in the ensuing melee before the other Farquharsons ran off, Robert Farquharson was killed by a sword through the heart and his brother John was so grievously wounded that he died a few days later.

On hearing the news of the death of his two sons MacCombie flew into a rage and declared: 'If I were but twenty years younger I would thin out the Farquharsons south of the Cairn o Mount and have a life for every finger and toe of my dead lads.'

Yet he did not mount a punitive attack, leaving it to the courts to outlaw some the Farquharsons. His hand might have been stayed further by the fact that Robert Farquharson's widow, Helen Ogilvie, also approached the court and asked for protection from John McIntosh of Forther, McCombie Mor. From then onwards the feud began to fade, but for the rest of his days McCombie Mor mourned the death of his sons, and particularly the first-born, the Gentle Giant, John. When at last he died at Crandart in Glenisla he left orders for his body to be taken and buried beside his beloved sons at Drumgley.

A Revenger's Tale

By the eighteenth century the clan system was in decline. The old ties of blood and kin were weakening with the influence of the money economy and increasing government attempts to open up the Highlands to outside influence. By the 1730s General Wade had started creating the network of metalled roads throughout the Highlands that was to allow the free movement of government troops in the years of the final Jacobite rebellion. Many chiefs had turned their backs on centuries of tradition and were becoming more like the landlords of England who felt nothing but contempt for those who paid the rents on their lands. An ancient way of life was coming to an end, and there were those who tried to hang on to the old ways as long as they could. One of these was a group of Highlanders who called themselves the Grampian Hunters. They had all been born into one or other of the many clachans that dotted the magnificent glens and straths of the Highlands, but many of them had been forced to work in the Lowlands. Some worked as drovers and others as smiths and other craftsmen, and few of them still lived in the clan-lands where their ancestors had dwelt so long. They would work through the winter months, but once the better weather of late spring came round they would meet up and move away to live in the hills till the snows began to threaten, at which point they would return to the lower glens and the Lowlands. With the disintegration of the clan system, there were increasingly areas of the Highlands that were virtually deserted and here they would live, spending much of their time in hunting.

Some of them, by the time of our story, were well advanced in years and had taken part in the cattle-raiding practices of the School of the Moon as young men. The life they lived in those summers was in some ways like that of the Fianna, the followers of Finn MacCoul whose legendary exploits formed the basis of so much poetry and song within the Gaeltacht. Traditionally, young men had often gone off hunting and raiding in just such bands. Most of them knew fine that the old ways had gone forever, but they held on to what they could, and when Prince Charlie raised his standard at Glenfinnan in 1745 they were happy to flock to follow the Jacobite cause. After that tragic episode the Grampian Hunters were never heard of more.

However, in the years before the '45 they were active in their beloved Highlands. One year, somewhere in the hills above the Angus Glens and south of the Dee they were joined by a young man from the West. He was a fine handsome specimen of a Highlander, strong and fit and a fine shot. He said he was a Maclan, and the younger son of a chief who had been driven away from his own people by the jealousy of his brothers. No one there had any reason to doubt him, and over that summer he showed himself to be a fine athlete in the various games and feats of strength with which they amused themselves. He also showed himself to be a natural leader of men. When the time came for the group to disband he went with some of the Grants back to Donside where he found work for the winter with a local smith. Here he married a local girl and seemed to be settling in to the community well. When the yellow was on the broom again and the call of the hills rose in the men's hearts, he left his young bride and made for the hills with the rest of the men. Some of the shielings were still in use, with cattle being brought up to fatten on the rich summer meadows of the high glens, so they were never out of contact for long, but mainly they spent their time living much the same as the ancient warrior bands had.

Maclan by now was so popular amongst the men that they had no hesitation in choosing him for their chief that year. It was in late August when they were camped in the hills above Glen Tanar after a few days of very successful hunting. They were sitting around their fire eating roast venison and drinking first-class home-made beer for which they had earlier traded some of their catch. All were intent on eating when suddenly a a shout was heard.

'Ewan of Dungyle,' the voice roared.

Maclan sprang to his feet as if he had been bitten by an adder and looked wildly round. Striding down from the slope of Mount Keen came a big old man, his long matted hair and beard completely grey. Old he might have been, and dressed in little more than rags, but he was still a great giant of a man. Round his waist was a crude girdle of goatskin, and sticking through it an ancient dirk. The wild man strode straight up to Maclan, who stood there, the blood having drained from his face.

'What do you want?' he asked in a quavering voice.

'Ewan of Dungyle, traitor to the most sacred trust. Your time has now come,' and so saying the old man whipped the dirk from his belt.

'You are a madman,' stuttered Maclan, stepping back from the naked blade.

'And who has made me mad but you,' roared the old man, and lunged at him.

Several of the others leapt at them and held him back, but it took all their strength to hold him. And all the time the old man's eyes were firmly fixed on the pale-faced Maclan.

'We do not know who you are,' said one of the men, called Hardy, 'but you are trying to attack one of our own.'

'Aye,' broke in another, by the name of Robertson, 'whoever you think you are after it is not our good friend Maclan.'

'Aye,' Hardy spoke again, 'if you do not agree to stop this attack and leave here this minute we will tie you up and leave you here on the hillside for the eagles and the ravens.'

At this a grim smile broke across the stranger's lips.

'Och, I am too near my prey now to be gainsaid,' he spoke softly, 'there stands the object of my vengeance and all the powers of earth and hell can no longer save him.'

At that he burst free from the grasp of the men holding him, lunged at Maclan and buried the blade of his dirk into the young man's heart. Maclan fell dead in the heather.

Hardy and the others unsheathed their own dirks and were about to fall on the wild stranger when he held up his left hand.

'Wait,' he shouted, 'hear me out, and if you do not accept what I say, you may kill me here. I will not resist.'

Hardy spoke, 'This had better be good old man.'

But he lowered his upraised hand and his companions did the same. And there above Glen Tanar, with the body of the young man lying in the heather, the old man told his story.

'This dirk,' he said, holding the weapon high and looking at it with a great sadness, 'took the life of my son when it was in the hands of that,' and he pointed at the corpse at his feet: 'This is how it came about.'

The old man had been a chieftain in Skye. He had just the one son, for his mother had died in childbirth and the old man had loved her dearly. So dearly that he never wanted to have anything to do with any other woman. So he doted on his only son, who reminded him so much of his beautiful mother, and the boy grew up fit and well. His closest companion was Ewan of Dungyle, brought up as his foster-brother in the chief's house. He had refused to let his son be brought up in another family but brought the son of an old friend to be his foster-brother. They had grown up as close as two lads could ever be, the old man told the assembled men on the hill. Now the old chieftain had a niece, a beautiful and gentle girl called Marianne, the daughter of his wife's sister, who was often about the house. She and his son had been sweethearts since they were but children and he had set his heart on them being married. Dispensation was given by the church for the union and the wedding date was set.

Plans were being laid for a major celebration when, just days before the wedding his son, Lachlan, disappeared. No one had any idea of where he could have gone, but foul play is suspected. Search-parties were sent all over the island and Ewan himself hardly slept for days. But no sign of Lachlan could be found. Marianne was beside herself with grief. One night the old chieftain called on Marianne to comfort her. They were sitting quietly by the fire in her home, talking gently, when the house was attacked by armed men. Hearing the commotion he ran to the window and looked out. There was a large group of armed men, all dressed in black and not a clan badge or any sign of who they could be. The men of the house were fighting them off, but the numbers were against them. Just as the old chief ran to help a cry went up inside the house, 'Fire, fire!' Somehow, someone had set fire to the building. The chief and the few men there sallied out against their foes. The black-dressed men fell back a few paces and it was obvious they outnumbered the people in the house by at least seven to one. At a muttered command several of the attackers raised muskets and fired. The old chief felt a ball whistle by his ear and heard a groan behind him. He turned in time to see Marianne fall back in the doorway of the burning house. Letting out a mighty roar he rushed at the attackers, striking several of them down, only to be felled by a blow from behind.

When he came to he was lying before the burning shell of the house, everyone else from the house lying on the ground in the flickering light of the flames. He got up on one knee and half crawled to where Marianne lay. One look told him she was dead, as were all of the occupants of the house, except one older woman who lay close to Marianne. She was whispering, and he crept over to listen to her last few faint breaths.

'It was Ewan of Dungyle, his mask slipped as he bent over Marianne . . .,' so saying, the poor woman died.

The chief returned home to recuperate, but he sent parties all over the island to look for Dungyle. Not a trace of him, or the men who were with him, could be found. He had clearly fled the island. Once he recovered enough to get about the old man himself began looking. He searched in all of the out-of-the-way places he could think of from his own youth, when he had explored the island, and on one of his trips he made a dreadful discovery. He found Lachlan's body in a deep cave with a dirk – the dirk he had wielded himself so recently – still stuck through his chest. His need for vengeance cried even stronger and he vowed never to rest till he had taken the life of the traitor Dungyle. From then on he never slept in the same bed twice, and spent summer and winter scouring Scotland for the traitor. He lived at times on little more than berries, hunting when he could and slowly spending the little silver money he had. He had terrified children and adults in clachans and villages all over the Highlands in his wanderings, looking, ever looking, for some sign of the foul traitor.

'Time and again I have walked through churches in the middle of sermons, silencing even the ministers and priests as I searched for this fiend,' the old man said, his voice growing softer. 'There was nothing for me in the words I heard. I have long forgotten any hopes of peace or happiness. But now I am revenged and the souls of Lachlan and Marianne may rest a little easier. Now I will lay myself down on the hillside and trouble no man more.'

And saying that, he threw down the blood-encrusted dirk and headed towards the woods on the ridge above. Behind him the Grampian Hunters could only watch in silence as he disappeared, never again to be seen by human eye. Then with an ill will they gathered together stones and raised a cairn over the man they had thought a true and honest friend.

BIRLINN LTD (incorporating John Donald and Polygon) is one of Scotland's leading publishers with over four hundred titles in print. Should you wish to be put on our catalogue mailing list **contact**:

Catalogue Request
Birlinn Ltd
West Newington House
10 Newington Road
Edinburgh EH9 1QS
Scotland, UK

Tel: + 44 (0) 131 668 4371
Fax: + 44 (0) 131 668 4466
e-mail: info@birlinn.co.uk

Postage and packing is free within the UK. For overseas orders, postage and packing (airmail) will be charged at 30% of the total order value.

For more information, or to order online, visit our website at **www.birlinn.co.uk**

Birlinn